PANDEMIC TO PEACE

Your Journey to Health, Wealth, Peace and Happiness

MITESH PATEL

UNI Publishing

PANDEMIC TO PEACE

Contents

Dedication		vii
1	The Pandemic	1
2	The Happiest Place on Earth	5
3	The UNI	12
4	Shenandoah National Park	20
5	The Law	31
6	Bells and Whistles	40
7	Awareness	56
8	Meditation	68
9	Co-creation	74
10	Media	84
11	Opinions and Approval	96
12	Health	112
13	Addictions	148
14	Brahma Shakti	160
15	Eternal Peace	178
Epilogue		201
About The Author		203

Copyright © 2020 by UNI Publishing

All rights reserved

No part of this book may be reproduced, or stored in a retrieval system, or transmitted in any form or by any means, electronic, mechanical, photocopying, recording, or otherwise, without express written permission of the publisher.

The author of this book does not dispense medical advice nor prescribe the use of any technique as a form of treatment for physical or mental problems without the advice of a physician or health care professional either directly or indirectly. The intent of the author is only to offer information of a general nature to help you in your quest for spiritual, emotional, and physical wellbeing. In the event you use any of the information in this book for yourself, the author and the publisher assume no responsibility for your actions.

ISBN-13: 978-1-7359652-1-5

Cover design by: germancreative
Library of Congress Control Number: 2018675309
Printed in the United States of America

Dedicated to peace for all mankind, for there is not enough. We are in desperate need of it and God knows we deserve it!

I

The Pandemic

"*Apparently this was all a setup though. It's all Antifa's agenda to divide and conquer us. Of course, we all fell for it, yet again.*" said my friend in response to the viral video of George Floyd, which all of us had watched recently. His arms were already crossed, eyebrows pulled down, upper and lower eyelids pulled up, lips tightened, showing clear signs of anger and defensiveness. I did not need to be a body language expert to read how he was feeling. The anger in his voice was a dead giveaway.

"*Everything is fake news to you Conspiritards! When you are this brainwashed, you can't see the truth even if it is right in front of your eyes. Why do you think Germans couldn't see Hitler's genocide?*" Fired back another friend. Her tone was one of disbelief with a hint of disgust.

It was on from that point and the rest of the evening was a wash!

I watched our friends passionately attack each other and defend their political beliefs. One side tried to educate the other on Obamagate, Pizzagate, the deep-state, fake news, Q'Anon, pedophilia rings, Jeffrey Epstein, Hollywood, and more.

However, the other side was also prepared to argue their case. They retorted back with accusations of racism, bigotry, brainwashing, cultism, narcissism, Dunning-Kruger effect, gaslighting, fearmongering, misinformation, dog-whistles, and more.

It has been over 24 hours since I watched the video of the events leading to George's death and then watched my friends fight in response to that video. I did not sleep well last night as a result of this disturbance. I love these friends! They are good people. We have helped each other and looked out for each other over the years. We have traveled and made memories together. We have had countless socials and laughs together.

Yet, yesterday's events were a sad reminder of the fact that we are not just racially divided but also politically divided in America. I miss the times when my friends used to be just friends. Now they are either "Republican Friends" or "Democrat Friends". It has been an exhausting four years for people like us who are neither "Conservatives" nor "Liberals".

Have we not been through enough?

The global pandemic, loss of millions of jobs, a devastated economy, conflict, chaos, violence, and of course the death toll of over a million lives and climbing.

I know many people believe that the pandemic is a hoax, that the death toll and unemployment numbers are inflated, and even that George's death was a setup. Believe what you wish, but we can all agree that the effects of the pandemic on our lives are very real.

Can anyone deny that the quarantine orders were issued, businesses were closed, millions were furloughed, masks had to be worn, the stimulus was issued, protests and riots plagued the world, shops burned, statues fell and at least a few people died during this chaos?

My mind is racing out of control with these thoughts.

Just about everyone is on the edge these days. People are angry...strike that, I am angry... strike that, I am outraged!

hoo-h'HOO-hoo-hoo...

A distinct sound wails through the air and I almost failed to register it in my state of anger. Then I heard it again...

hoo-h'HOO-hoo-hoo....

then again...

hoo-h'HOO-hoo-hoo.... most definitely an owl hooting in the middle of the day!

"Oh, thank God! That is my signal. They've found me! Here in the middle of Leu Gardens on a hot summer day in Orlando, they've found me" I exclaimed.

But why am I surprised that they have found me in my time of need? They can find me anywhere on this planet or even in this solar system. The most clandestine agency simply known as "UNI" (pronounced: *yoo-nee* or *you-an-i*) has more resources at its disposal than all the governments on this planet, combined. Their communication & tracking technology is lightyears ahead of anything publicly available on this planet. They have always found me in my time of need and delivered to me exactly what I have hired them to deliver; health, wealth, happiness, and peace!

Now that the UNI agent has located and made contact with me, all will be well again. With that knowingness, my heart filled with warmth, and I felt so blessed to be one of the very few individuals fortunate enough to be under the protection of the UNI, during these incredibly trying and chaotic times.

What is "UNI" and how do you hire them?

2

The Happiest Place on Earth

I wake up when my eyes open, I go to sleep when my heart desires, and everything in between is on my terms.

I cannot even remember the last time I used an alarm to wake me up in the morning. My alarm is nature itself. I generally wake up to the soothing sounds of this sweet...sweet mockingbird outside my window. This little bird loves to show off its wide range of vocal abilities including its rendition of a car alarm. Love that bird!

As I reemerge into this body every morning, I take a few moments to appreciate the peaceful night of sleep and how refreshed my body feels. I turn around and see the beautiful face of the most loving person I have ever known, my wife. After a brief period of playfulness with her, I am ready to jump off the bed and start another day of adventures!

The living room almost always greets us with gentle morning sun and breeze passing through the panoramic windows. I begin by writing a letter to my friend and then it is time for some exercise. I prefer yoga, stretching or light exercise in the morning and my wife prefers rebounding. After exercising, we come to the big question, what is for breakfast? Breakfast is a ritual for us and so is every meal of the day. We look forward to the mealtimes and get excited about it like it is Christmas morning and breakfast is our gift! Our meals are always delicious and super nutritious.

Is it time for work after breakfast?

Yeah, right!

The next big question of the day is, which lake are we walking to today? The beautiful state of Florida has over 30,000 lakes and we are blessed with a few within walking distance. Our walks to the lake are always invigorating, and a special time for us to count the blessings in our lives. I actively recall and state what I am grateful for on my way to the lake and my wife takes her turn on the way back. While we sit at the lake, something unexpected, delightful, and visually pleasing generally happens.

Is it time for work now?

Maybe. Once we return from the walk and shower, it is time to consider work, if we feel like it. When we do work, we easily accomplish at least 10 hours worth of work, within a short time. This is possible because we use the UNI resources for most of the heavy lifting. Sometimes it feels wrong to let them do all the hard work, but the guilt passes quickly.

Lunchtime is next!

While my wife prepares a hot delicious meal with care and love, my task is to prepare a beverage for us. The beverage of choice is either a home-brewed "flavor of the month" Kombucha or something else full of probiotics. My wife generally does not reveal what she is making for lunch because she loves to surprise me. Although, I have become good at figuring it out, just based on the mouth-watering aroma rising from the kitchen. I still act surprised even when I know. Her cooking is always delicious and nourishing.

What happens after lunch is one of my favorite activities of the day!

We take about an hour after lunch to meditate. At the end of these meditations, we are always refreshed and energized. Once we finish our meditation, we are free to play for the rest of the day. The UNI team will take care of the tasks to ensure businesses keep running and money keeps flowing while we head out for an evening of fun. Our evening generally includes engaging in one of the thousands of fun activities Orlando has to offer. The joy we feel as the evening approaches is the joy children feel when the homework is done and it is playtime!

What will it be today?

Would it be the wizarding world of Harry Potter at Universal Studios or would I play "Ikran Makto" with my mountain banshee at Disney's Animal Kingdom?

From Fun Spot America to factory outlets, dining to dancing, theme parks to theaters, nature to nightlife, beach to a balloon ride; the options are abundant. We have the time, money, and energy to do whatever our hearts desire, every evening. More importantly, we have the freedom to do what we want. It has been four years since we moved to Orlando and we are still loving all it has to offer. Before the pandemic, at least twice a week, we used to end our magical day with enchanting sights and sounds of the fireworks spectacular at the "Happiest Place on Earth", Disney that is!

Since my retirement before the age of 40, we have been living this carefree life of our choosing and design. A few years before that, we were traveling to about 30 cities a year and building my tech company. And a few years from now, we will change many aspects of our lives again, for the gypsy spirit in us will always continue to desire the next best thing. Whether there is a pandemic, protest, or political upheaval, our playtime is protected by our powerful partner, the UNI. Our fun, even in times of turmoil is guaranteed by our agreement with the UNI.

How is it possible for a formerly homeless immigrant to live this life?

It is possible because I discovered the UNI during my arduous journey from homelessness to happiness and started working with them. While how I went from homeless to happy is not the focus of this book, I would give you a little summary to set the stage.

I landed in America on Tax Day, April 15th, 1995. I had just finished high school in India and was getting ready for college when my family was presented with the opportunity to send me to America. The problem was, I did not speak English or know much about America. This was the time when computers and the internet were still in their infancy, and Google, texting, messaging, smartphones and social media did not exist. Access to information was very primitive and international communication was very difficult. Sending an 18-year old to a foreign country was much scarier than it is today.

Therefore, my father took measures to ensure I would be safe. He made a deal with my Uncle who had lived in America most of his life. The deal was that my Uncle will look after me and help me go to college and I will pay him back generously when I am able. I was a quick study and good at school. Therefore, no one had any doubts that I would do well in life and pay him back generously. Making a deal like this is common among immigrants, so it did not raise any concerns.

What we did not know was that my Uncle had a vested interest in a Motel in Georgia, which was in financial trouble. They needed a slave to labor for free and an 18-year old who did not speak English or have the wherewithal to survive in America was a perfect candidate.

So, I ended up in that rundown Motel on exit 69 of I-75, slaving from early morning to late night for a can of soda and a meal. I could not contact my family because making international calls was not possible from the Motel rooms and because of my limited communication skills, I was unable to ask for help from any guests at the Motel. After many months of relentless labor, I was exhausted and malnourished. My hopes and dreams were almost dead.

Yet the fighter inside lived on and hatched an escape plan. First, I had to learn English. So, I would take the free newspapers from the Motel, attempt to read them, and highlight the words I did not understand. I would look up those words in my English to Gujarati (my native language) dictionary and memorize them. I would also listen to the TV in my room and repeat the lines out loud to improve my accent. In due time, I was having basic conversations with guests at the Motel. My ability to converse with the guests threatened my oppressors. They progressively became more aggressive in their control, threats, and manipulations. My ability to communicate made me more confident and I gradually started resisting their oppression. On one stormy night at that Motel in Chula, Georgia, the oppressors took a final jab at me to crush my spirit. The oppressors had a plan to scare me straight on that night. They had fabricated false accusations to get me locked-up unless I agreed to comply with all their demands going forward. It was good old-fashioned extortion. Instead of complying, I asked them to have me locked up in the hopes that I would be free of my slavery when I get out of jail.

So, my Uncle picked up the phone and pretended to dial 9-1-1. Surprisingly, he hung up after a few seconds and claimed that the line was busy. Even I knew that 9-1-1 was not going to be busy in that sleepy little town of Chula, Georgia. In my naiveté, I had unintentionally called their bluff. They knew it and I knew it. Frustrated by the failure of their devious plot, they threw me out of the Motel on that stormy night with only the clothes I was wearing. They had hoped that being homeless and helpless on a stormy night would scare me enough to come back begging.

They were wrong!

That night I became homeless but something inside me was awakened for the first time! I was finally free, had a chance at survival, and I was going to fight for it with my last breath!

By this time, my English had improved enough to work a job at McDonald's at approximately $4 per hour. It was not enough to survive but enough to get me from living behind a dumpster to a roach-infested cheap Motel room in a nearby town of Tifton, Georgia. I quickly took additional jobs to survive. I picked up a night shift at a manufacturing plant and also worked at a convenience store. Most of my time was spent working and the rest to improve my English and learn the ways of America. Simply by observing others, I learned how to buy groceries, pump gas, order food, and everything else. It was tremendous hardwork but I loved being free so much that I was happy to do it. The holidays were usually quite lonely, but I found comfort in observing other families enjoying themselves at the mall and hoped that someday I too, will find joy.

In due time, two other Uncles learned about my misfortune and offered me shelter and support. With their kindness and my savings from the labor jobs, I obtained much-needed education, which resulted in my first professional job.

It was through hard work and perseverance that I had survived modern slavery. Ultimately, my habit of hard-work became the norm. By the year 2006, life was relatively good. I was married, lived in Princeton, New Jersey and I had finally found not just joy, but also love!

However, my troubles were not over yet.

I had a good management job, and I was building a business on the side. I had poured my time, money, and efforts into developing cutting-edge technology with great potential and I was working all waking hours, 7 days a week. I had partnered with an experienced executive to help with the management of this new venture. I was generous enough to give him about half of the equity in the company. My life was all work and not much play and I was starting to burnout.

To make the matters worse, the executive I had partnered with turned out to be an alcoholic and a crook. He embezzled money, repelled customers, and did everything to destroy the company. The money was gone, the company was derailed, and I would have to take legal action or lose the company. My life was a mess once again!

"I am a good person, I have never done anything to harm anyone, why did I end up with this horrible business partner?" I screamed in anger one late night as I instinctively looked up at the sky in the hopes that God was listening.

"Why do you put me through these horrible experiences. All I want is a good life and to be happy. If you exist, show me the way!" I shouted out loud furiously.

Soon after that night, I found the UNI.

3

The UNI

"I'm still waiting for my audios to finish downloading and then I'll hit the road", I told my wife as I stared out the window of my office. She was wondering where I was and had called to check on me. It was getting late in the evening and most of the employees had left already. I worked at a major pharmaceutical company in Edison, NJ. Like most jobs, it was a routine nine to five thing and I was in a rut, just like most employees. However, this evening was different because I was so excited to be flying out the next day for a weeklong Caribbean vacation. Ever since we got married, we tried to get away together as much as possible. I loved nothing more than going away to the Caribbean islands and disconnecting from work. During the flight, I enjoyed listening to random audiobooks to kill time. As an IT professional, I was no stranger to peer-to-peer networks where I could get my hands on the most exciting content, unavailable to the public. As I was secretly browsing the back alley of the internet, a mysterious title of an audio set immediately caught my attention. So, I started downloading it without really knowing what I was getting myself into.

"What in the world is this?" I thought as I continued listening to the audios on my flight the next day. As I listened to the esoteric nature of the audios, I felt like Morpheus would materialize out of thin air at any moment and say to me, *"whereas the red pill ... you stay in wonderland, and I show you how deep the rabbit hole goes."* I have always loved the Matrix movies and I thought I was about to experience my own real-life "red pill" moment...and I did!

Just as young aspiring astrophysics student, Casey Newton (Britt Robinson), stumbles upon the secret invitation when she is given a mysterious pin by a youth named Athena (Raffey Cassidy) in the movie Tomorrowland, I had stumbled upon my real-life invitation to meet the UNI. I was about to be recruited by the most powerful agency on the planet and I was clueless about it. My life was about to change forever, and I did not even know it. However, I knew something unusual was taking place within me. My body had turned into a cocktail of mixed emotions as I continued listening to the audios. I knew I was venturing into very unknown territory by getting involved with the UNI yet **something about it felt right** and I took the plunge

Now, with well over a decade of working with the UNI, I will categorically say that meeting the UNI was the best thing that ever happened to me! I went from an employee stuck in a dead-end job to starting my own companies to retired before age 40. I went from financial worries to financial freedom. I went from worrying about jobs, bills, money, marriage, children, current events, politics, religion, future, health, and even death to living a completely carefree and peaceful life. I sleep in peace when the day is done, and I finally know what it means to be happy.

If you have not figured it out already, this book is **your invitation to meet UNI.**

As a faithful, proven and loyal member of the UNI organization, I am allowed to introduce the UNI to others. While I have introduced the UNI to people I have mentored, I have never felt the urge to speak about the UNI on a mass scale. I have seen what the pandemic has done to my friends, this beautiful country I call home (America), and the world. If it had not been for the suffering of mankind as a result of the pandemic, I would never be willing to invite anyone else. This book is a public invitation for those that are ready to take control. Those that want a life of their choosing and will not settle for anything less. Just the fact that you are reading this book, you have taken your first step towards meeting the UNI. But, let me make it clear that there is no such thing as a free lunch. **While the UNI will work with you regardless of your race, religion, nationality, financial status, intellect, or gender, you must qualify first. Some rules must be followed and some sacrifices must be made to work with the UNI.**

Are you ready?

Before we go any further, let us first find out if your communication equipment is working properly. Working with the UNI is not possible if your apparatus can not communicate with them properly. As I mentioned previously, the UNI communication & tracking technology is lightyears ahead of anything publicly available on this planet. The UNI communication technology does not work with satellite, radio, or cellular signals due to the limitations of such signals. The UNI wanted to ensure they can track and communicate with anyone, anywhere, and at any time. Therefore, they have infused their communication technology directly into the Prana, the energy that powers all living beings. By doing so, the UNI ensures continuous communication with you, as long as you are alive.

Hard to believe, isn't it?

This may be the correct time to inform you that this book contains esoteric knowledge which by definition is likely to be understood by only a small number of people. I know what you are reading may seem foreign or farfetched and it will certainly challenge your belief system. Nonetheless, I ask for you to open your mind to the realm of possibilities. This knowledge has transformed my life and I hope to share that with you. As a reader learning about this for the first time, you may feel very skeptical. However, do not force yourself to continue reading if the information does not resonate with you after a chapter or two. I have mentored enough people to know that this information will resonate so well with many people but will have an adverse reaction on some others. Both reactions are expected but only the people that this resonates with can understand, apply and benefit from such information. If everyone could understand what wealthy, healthy, or happy people understand, we would only have wealthy, healthy, and happy people in the world. That is certainly not the case. The fact is not everyone can understand everything and that is perfectly fine, too.

Shall we continue?

Every human is already equipped with the UNI Communication System (UCS). You may not know it because no one has ever told you about it. Just like your cell signal, Prana energy is also invisible to the naked eye. Just the way your cell phone receives the invisible cell signal, and the Operating System of your cell phone translates it into what you see or hear on your cell phone, your body receives the Prana energy infused with UNI communication and the UCS within your body, translates it. You already know that your cell signal strength varies depending on your location. Just like that, the UNI signal strength also varies at times but unlike the cell signal, it has nothing to do with your location. Imagine that you dropped your cell phone and something broke inside causing the signal to be distorted on your device. Now your broken phone is distorting the signal when you make calls or watch videos, even when you are standing next to a cell tower. Just like that, the UNI signal always reaches your body successfully but certain conditions within your body can distort what the UCS is telling you. **These bodily conditions include, but are not limited to, the influ-**

ence of alcohol or certain illegal drugs, certain health issues, certain prescription drugs, levels of toxins within your body, and most importantly, your emotional state, etc.

There is a simple test we can perform to identify if your body is receiving a clear signal at this moment or whether there is distortion. You may already be familiar with this test, especially if you work with alternative healing practices. Whether you know the test or not, just play along.

Are you ready?

- Change into comfortable clothes and remove any jewelry or watches from your body and empty your pockets.
- You will need a friend to help you with this test.
- Get two identical sticky notes or pieces of paper.
- Write the word "LOVE" on one of them and "HATE" on the other.
- Fold both sticky notes at least twice so that you cannot see the word written on them and do not mention what is written on the sticky notes to the friend helping you.
- Shuffle both notes enough so that they are mixed up and you have no way of knowing which one is which.
- Study the illustration below before you and your friend begin

- You will take the position of the woman in the illustration while holding ONE of the sticky notes in your fist. You should not know what is written on the note, neither should your friend.
- You will ask your friend to take the position of the man shown in Step 1.
- Your friend will try to push your hand down as shown in Step 2.
- Your job is to hold your hand up strongly and resist as your friend pushes it down. Your friend must apply enough force to overcome your resistance and push your hand down as shown in Step 2. The objective of this test is to identify how much force is required to push your hand down. Ask your friend to remember how much strength it took to push your hand down.
- Now put away the first sticky note and hold the second sticky note in your fist. Perform both steps again.

Ask your friend which sticky note required more strength to push your hand down.

Was it the first or the second?

Your test is successful if there is a clear difference in the amount of force required between the two notes. Do not read any further until you have completed this test.

***

Once you have completed the test, feel free to open the sticky notes, and identify which one made you strong and which one made you weak.

Are you surprised that holding the sticky note with the word "LOVE" written on it makes you strong while the word "HATE" makes you weak?

If your results were ambiguous or reversed, then you are not receiving a clear UNI signal due to distortion. No worries, I will show you how to deal with distortion and boost your signal throughout this book and especially in the "Health" chapter. You may have some questions regarding this test.

How did my body know what was written on the note I was holding?

The UNI told your body what was written on the note.

How did the UNI know I was performing this test? I did not do anything to alert the UNI?

Well, if you think Big Brother is always watching you, think again. **Every part of your body is in constant communication with the UNI.** They always know exactly what is going on with you. The UNI knows you better than your spouse or your parents. **The UNI knows you better than you know yourself.** They know everything about you including your every thought and every desire! Yes, even your dirty desires are known to the UNI. However, there is no reason to be concerned about it. The UNI will never judge, embarrass, blackmail, harass, or harm you. Those are human tendencies and for an agency as powerful as the UNI, they are above such petty human tendencies. Besides, you agreed to have the UCS installed in your body just the way you agreed to the terms and conditions of your cell phone provider. You could not use the cell phone unless you agreed to the terms and conditions. Just like that, you could not use a human body unless you agree to have the UCS installed and activated within the body.

There is a reason why UNI can also be pronounced "You-an-I" because **your relationship with the UNI is the most intimate relationship you will ever have in your life.** It has always been that way. You simply did not know about it until now.

Why would I have ever agreed to have the UCS installed in my body and spy on me?

4

Shenandoah National Park

"You got lucky," said the elderly man sitting in a rocking chair right outside the historic Big Meadows Lodge in the Shenandoah National Park. I was sipping on a delicious Meadow Mule and overlooking the gorgeous valley when he spoke to me. I suspected that he was delivering a message from the UNI

"How so?" I asked the man to continue further verification.

"There was a big storm headed this way, it changed direction at the last minute and went further away from Shenandoah. You got lucky with this good weather today," concluded the elderly man.

"How else would it be? I'm the luckiest man you will ever meet!" I chuckled, now certain that he was delivering a message from the UNI. Most people think weather control is a conspiracy theory. When you work with UNI, weather management is just another one of many perks available to you. Ever since I started working with the UNI, my important plans never had to suffer because of inclement weather. The UNI will alter the weather as necessary to make sure my plans and experiences are not interrupted. For the UNI, changing the weather is as simple as changing the thermostat in your house is for you. I was not kidding when I said, the UNI has more resources at its disposal than all the governments on this planet, combined.

After some initial pleasantries, my wife and I continued chatting with the elderly man to further reveal the message from the UNI, *"You can stay at the historic Natural Bridge Hotel on your way down. It gives you walking access to the Natural Bridge. The bridge is majestic. If you want more, you can hike to the waterfall and even to the caverns. You can easily spend a day or two there and I am sure you will love it"* said the elderly man.

What seems like a normal conversation between two people was actually a specific message from the UNI to let us know where to stop next and what to do. The UNI agents have been guiding us along the way on this road trip because that is what we had asked for while planning this trip with the UNI.

"Make it fun! I want to see my Mom and family. I want to remember my time with her. We also want to see some friends, make lots of memories, eat, drink, and laugh together. We want lots of good food and fresh delicious fruits. We want to see cool sites, experience nature, breathe fresh air, and hike the trails along the way. We want only good experiences. We want empty roads, flowing traffic, and courteous drivers. We want to be safe the entire trip and maintain our peace and happiness. We do not care to plan everything upfront, so prepare us for impromptu adventures and guide us along the way as you see fit."

Those were the instructions we gave to the UNI team regarding our upcoming road trip. The main purpose of the trip was to see my elderly mother, who was dealing with a health challenge. She lives near Bear Mountain in the state of New York, which was the hardest-hit with the pandemic at the time of planning this trip. Virtually everyone was paralyzed with fear at the time. Instead of flying, we chose to drive so we could make this a road trip to remember and have lots of fun along the way. Just like everyone else, the state of Florida was in quarantine for over a month and our options for fun activities in Orlando were reduced. This was unacceptable to our gypsy spirit. Therefore, going on a fun road trip sounded like the next logical thing for us. Most people would be worried about making such a long road trip during a raging pandemic. We were not worried at all. We knew that all we had to do is **communicate clearly** what we wanted to the UNI and they would plan every detail of it. We knew that there would not be any chance of us getting sick as we are under the protection of the UNI. So, we shamelessly presented our list of demands to the UNI.

Note: Throughout this book, I will sometimes refer to the UNI as a group ("them") and other times as an entity. Both references are accurate as the UNI represents both a group and an entity.

I was not always so shameless in my demands. I was quite shy when I first started working with the UNI. I was not born into a rich family and had to work very hard for everything in my life. Nothing was ever handed to me. My first few years in America were very tumultuous. When I first started working with the UNI, I was told that **I can be, do or have anything I wanted** as long as I **follow the rules and make some sacrifices**. I had reviewed the rules and they were not too difficult to follow. If anything, the rules are much harder to believe than to follow. Once you **believe in the rules** even if you do not understand the reason for them, following them is easy. The sacrifices, on the other hand, are so much harder to make. But I wanted the "Good Life" so badly that I was willing to make any sacrifice for it. Because of my modest upbringing and struggles in life, I was quite shy in my asking at first. I settled with little requests like finding parking right in front of the Triumph Brewing Company or Winberries in Princeton downtown on a Friday night. Usually, it was nearly impossible to find a parking spot there on Friday nights when the entire college town came out to have fun. I was blown away when the UNI delivered my first parking spot exactly as expected! The UNI works in very subtle and clandestine ways to maintain a low profile. For example, they will not block the parking spot with an orange cone and "Reserved" sign as it would attract attention. Instead, they will have an agent parked in the spot reserved for me until I arrived. The agent would pull out as soon as my car approached. The best thing about UNI is the amusing ways in which they make things happen for you. Enjoying the best parking spots everywhere became a regular occurrence since then. As time passed, I became bolder in my demands and very soon, I was shameless enough to ask for $50,000 without having to work for it.

How do you think that turned out?

Soon after I requested the $50,000, the CEO of a company I had helped long ago, showed up at my door with a $50,000 check to my name. He gave me that money for having introduced him to a business contact via email. Apparently, that introduction turned into a lucrative deal for the company and the CEO wanted to thank me with exactly $50,000; not a penny more, not a penny less...exactly $50,000.

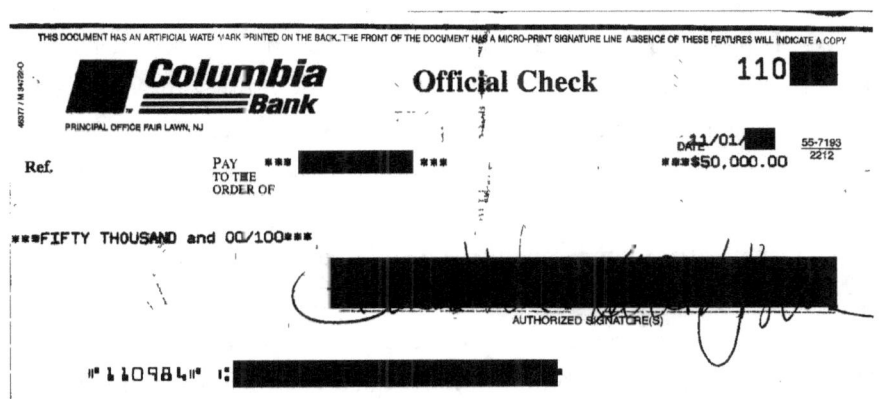

Wouldn't you love to make $50,000 for writing one email?

That was about a decade ago when I received my $50,000 check.

Since then I have become much better at working with the UNI and my results commensurate with my skills. It did not take long to go from manifesting fifty thousand to manifesting millions of dollars with ease. I wanted to include the check for millions in this book as well but was prevented by a non-disclosure requirement. I am generally reasonable in my demands because I understand that not much is required to be happy. However, some of the others that work with the UNI are much bolder in their demands. Anytime you see someone achieving awe-inspiring results, they are likely working with the UNI. I had the privilege of meeting some of these overachievers of our times. Once you have experience working with the UNI, you will be able to identify others that also work with the UNI.

* * *

I looked around the historic Big Meadows Lodge in the Shenandoah National Park. The original lodge was built in 1939 with stones cut from the Massanutten Mountain and the entire interior structure of the lodge, including the paneling, is made from native chestnut trees, which today are virtually extinct. The lodge is listed on the National Register of Historic Places. Shenandoah National Park is one of my favorite places. It has 197,438.76 acres of wilderness housing over 60 peaks that have an elevation of over 3,000 feet and 105 miles of Skyline Drive with over 75 amazing overlooks. My wife and I have enjoyed virtually all the overlooks of Skyline Drive. We have pictures taken at most of them.

It was day thirteen of our three-week road trip which was planned entirely by the UNI. Everything had been amazing and better than expected so far. Mom was doing better and seeing the family was pleasant. We picnicked at Bear Mountain, barbequed by the pool, and splashed everyone by making a large wave pool. Even with her health challenges, Mom overfed me every day with my childhood favorites. I had seven-course meals every day. Most of the women in my family are incredible cooks and my Mom is the queen of the culinary arts. Mom also packed tons of food for the road as we had departed a few days ago. Nothing tastes better than Mom's munchies while you are on the road. Our cup of memories was already full and we were not done yet.

The previous night we had stayed at the Skyland lodge. As we left New York and headed towards Virginia, the UNI inspired us to take I-95 instead of I-81. Anyone who has traveled along these roads knows that I-81 is a scenic highway and a much better choice than I-95.

Why would the UNI send us down I-95 then?

Well, it became clear when we took a break to refuel and saw Biryani City restaurant. We picked up some food from there for our dinner. The very first bite of that Gobi Manchurian from Biryani City kicked off the party for my tastebuds. Having such a delicious meal while sitting on a patio, overlooking the valley below, made it that much more enjoyable. I mention these experiences, to show you the flawless ways in how the UNI was fulfilling our road-trip demands.

Skyland Lodge is nestled along miles 41.7 & 42.5 at Skyline Drive's highest elevation - 3,680 feet. The UNI had made sure we got the best views everywhere. The first night, we stayed at the Skyland lodge and the next day we moved to the Big Meadows Lodge for a true log cabin experience. We spent the day hiking a loop trail and climbing the Blackrock summit where we took some fun pictures.

I always wanted to hike in Shenandoah, have a meal at the Big Meadows Lodge, and sleep in a true log cabin. All those desires were fulfilled thanks to the impeccable planning of the UNI. **A life of your choosing is a life where your desires are fulfilled with ease.** I write this book to lead people away to lead you away from the trauma of the global pandemic, devastated economy, dirty politics, misinformation, civil unrest, and chaos. I aim to show people how to increase their Health, Wealth, Peace, and Happiness in any situation. This book will teach you **how to** work with the UNI to create a life of your choosing regardless of what is going on in the world around you.

Note: *We all know that pictures are better in color. No worries if you are reading this book in black & white. All color pictures in the order of appearance can be found here:* http://bit.ly/mybookpics

The first night, we stayed at the Skyland lodge and the next day we moved to the Big Meadows Lodge for a true log cabin experience. We spent the day hiking a loop trail and climbing the Blackrock summit where we took some fun pictures. I always wanted to hike in Shenandoah, have a meal at the Big Meadows Lodge, and sleep in a true log cabin. All those desires were fulfilled thanks to the impeccable planning of the UNI. **A life of your choosing is a life where your desires are fulfilled with ease.**

Did you know there was a raging pandemic, protests, and chaos out there?

Where I stayed, there was nothing but nature. No signs of chaos. Just Peace! **Peace is all about how you focus!**

PANDEMIC TO PEACE - 27

5

The Law

This is an important chapter as you can see by the title. There is a law that guides everything there is. This is how the law works:

What you focus on expands.
What you focus on with your five senses; touch, sight, smell, taste, and hearing; expands.
What you focus on with your thoughts, expands.
What you focus on with your emotions, expands.
What you focus on, with any part of your being, expands.
What you focus on with one or more parts of your being, expands.
The more parts you involve in your focus, the faster it expands.
As you get more beings to focus, the expansion becomes exponential.
The expansion has an energetic pull, like gravity or magnets.
The bigger the expansion, the stronger the pull.

This is the Law of Focus also known as the Law of Attraction. It has been "The Supreme Law" since the beginning, and it will be that for eternity. There are no exceptions to this law. **Since this is the supreme**

law, it forms the basis for all that is, and all that happens to you, your family, your neighborhood, your city, your county, your state, your country, and your world. The Law of Focus is responsible for managing everything. Therefore, all UNI systems are 100% in harmony with this law. This is why UNI systems always produce marvelous results.

If this is your first time hearing about the Law of Focus, you are in for a world of fascinating revelations. If you have already been introduced to the Law of Attraction, this book will take your understanding to another level by giving you another perspective on the matter.

You do not need to know what is under the hood of your car to reap the benefits of driving. Just like that, you do not need a detailed understanding of the Law of Attraction to reap the benefits of working with the UNI. This book will give you everything you need to know, to work with the UNI. Additionally, I will point you in the correct direction for those that are curious to know what is under the hood and want a detailed understanding of how things work behind the scene. You will find that information at the end of this book.

For the time being, fully internalize these statements:

What you focus on expands.
What you focus on with your five senses; touch, sight, smell, taste, and hearing; expands.
What you focus on with your thoughts, expands.
What you focus on with your emotions, expands.
What you focus on, with any part of your being, expands.
What you focus on with one or more parts of your being, expands.
The more parts you involve in your focus, the faster it expands.
As you get more beings to focus, the expansion becomes exponential.
The expansion has an energetic pull, like gravity or magnets.
The bigger the expansion, the stronger the pull.

Memorize those statements like your future depends on it, and it does. Let us review a real-life example of the Law of Focus and how it applies to relationships.

Jenna meets Jack and they fall in love. At the beginning of a relationship, most couples are so excited by each other and naturally focused on the positive qualities of each other. They are physically aroused by each other and the idea of spending time together is delicious. There is a sense of thrill and adventure in everything they do together. Everything feels better when romance is in the air. The first kiss, the first movie, the first walk on the beach, and of course; the first lovemaking. All the firsts are fantastic. You get the idea.

What happens later in the relationship?

Somewhere along the way, one or both will manage to focus on the first negative quality of the other person. Maybe it is the annoying smacking of Jack's lips when he chews food or how long it takes for Jenna to get ready. Let us assume for this example that Jenna focused on the annoying smacking sound Jack makes while chewing food. Jenna first became aware of it when she heard it at the dinner table. Her ears focused on it first. She then looked at Jack and focused on it with her eyes also. Now two of her senses are engaged in focusing on the smacking sound, so it expands faster. As she stared at him listening to his smacking, she thought, *"Why is he chewing like a pig? Does he not know manners? Was he raised in a barn?"*

So, now her thoughts have joined the party, and her eyes, ears, and thoughts; are all focused on the smacking. As she begins thinking those thoughts for the first time in her life, something interesting is happening in her brain. A new pattern of neurons begins to fire in her brain for the first time, corresponding to her negative thoughts. If Jenna continues to think and repeat such thoughts, dendrites will begin forming in her brain to connect the neurons, and therefore solidifying this new negative thought pattern into a neural pathway. In other words, Jenna's brain will make it easier for Jenna to keep thinking these negative thoughts if she does not stop in due time. Of course, it takes a lot of repetitions for the pattern to solidify and turn into a neural pathway, but that is where Jenna is heading.

Once you begin thinking about what you are focused upon, emotions will ensue in response to your thoughts. Emotions are either positive, negative, or neutral/ambiguous depending on your exact thoughts regarding what you are focused upon. Because Jenna is thinking negative thoughts, the resulting emotion will be negative. In this case, the emotion resulting from her thoughts will most likely be of annoyance. To induce annoyance in Jenna's body, a mild toxin gets produced in her body which Jenna will recognize as "annoyance".

Now Jenna's emotions have joined the party and she is focusing on the smacking with her eyes, ears, thoughts, and emotions. Remember, **what you focus on with one or more parts of your being, expands. The more parts you involve in your focus, the faster it expands.** Oh boy, this is getting interesting now.

Jenna has less than a minute to get out of this mess, but she does not know that because she is unaware of how the Law of Focus works. **If she continues to give her undivided attention to that newly found annoyance, the Law of Focus will begin the process of queueing up more annoying things for Jenna.** Jenna makes the mistake and continues to focus on the lip-smacking. Annoyed, she continues to stare at Jack's face, and the next thing she notices is the hair sticking out of Jack's nose. So, it begins with the nose hair now. The Law of Focus just provided another annoyance for Jenna to focus on.

Jenna begins to focus on the nose hair and starts thinking similar negative thoughts. Because her negative thoughts about the nose hair are similar to her negative thoughts about smacking, the resulting emotion will simply add to the intensity of annoyance, upgrading her annoyance to irritation. Not to mention that the toxicity in her body had to increase, to upgrade annoyance to irritation.

Remember how holding the word "HATE" in your hand made you weaker? Just like that, Jenna's body is now weaker due to the emotion of irritation. We have all been irritated enough to know that these toxins are mild and will not kill Jenna. That is true unless her focus continues in this direction for prolonged periods and upgrades to an emotion that has much higher levels of toxicity, such as hate. Reaching toxic levels of hate or rage for prolonged periods will most certainly impact Jenna's health, wellbeing, and happiness.

Luckily for our couple, Jack finished eating and got up to put the dishes away. Thank God the dinner is over. Now that Jack is not at the dinner table, Jenna's brain manages to focus on something else, like the meme she just received on her cell phone.

What happened to the expansion that took place because of Jenna's continued and undivided focus?

It is intact and available for future use. This expansion now has some magnetic pull of its own.

Remember the new neuron patterns that were created in Jenna's brain?

Let us assume Jenna had enough repetition of her negative thoughts to create a very basic neural pathway. In the beginning, this neural pathway will be weak, but if she continues thinking such negative thoughts repeatedly, more and more dendrites will be created, connecting more and more neurons. In other words, the neural pathway will become stronger and stronger. If that happens, thinking negative thoughts about Jack will become an automated habit and Jenna will be unable to stop it. Let us label this newly created weak neural pathway as "The Irritating Husband", which is now stored in Jenna's brain for future use.

It is not over for our couple just yet. The next day at Dinner, Jenna focuses on the smacking again as soon as Jack takes his very first bite.

Why so quickly?

Because "The Irritating Husband" neural pathway was available and ready for reuse. As soon as Jenna focused on the smacking, the neural pathway was activated instantly. Activating these patterns of neuronal firing immediately produces the toxin resulting in the negative emotion of irritation. That is not all. The expansion continues as well and **so does the magnetic pull of that expansion.**

As Jenna continues to focus on Jack's smacking night after night, three things are happening: 1) The neural pathway is becoming stronger and well defined. 2) The resulting emotion of irritation is becoming more intense heading towards upgrading itself to anger 3) The magnetic pull of the expansion is also increasing and pulling in other similar annoyances in Jenna's experience. Jenna is now aware of many more of Jack's annoyances. From burping to passing gas, nothing is unnoticed anymore. She has even started to notice similar annoyances in her coworkers and other people around her. This is because the expansion now has a lot more magnetic pull and the Law of Focus is pulling in more irritations in Jenna's experience. **This magnetic pull has some real consequences** as you will see later in this book.

Frustrated with Jack's smacking, Jenna seeks the advice of her BFF. She sets up a dinner with her BFF. Over this dinner, the two of them discuss all of Jack's irritations in detail. The BFF has her own irritation stories to add to the mix. In other words, now two beings are focused on the irritations. **As you get more beings to focus, the expansion be-**

comes exponential. At the end of that dinner, the two ladies conclude that Jenna should confront Jack about cleaning up his act. By this time, Jenna has successfully upgraded her irritation to anger.

Are you getting the sense of where this is heading?

The next day at the dinner table, Jenna jumps on the opportunity to expose Jack in front of their children. Now even the children are made aware of the issues and focusing on them. **As you get more beings to focus, the expansion becomes exponential.** Luckily for everyone, Jack agrees to monitor his chewing going forward to set a good example for his family. But this is not over yet.

Night after night as they gather at the dinner table, Jack is always under a microscope. He tries his best to avoid smacking, but old habits are hard to get rid of. If Jack slips, he gets a scolding from the family. Not to mention that every time he slips, everyone focuses on the smacking again and the expansion continues. Every time Jack is scolded, he can not help but have his own negative thoughts in reaction to the scolding.

"I'm the breadwinner in the family. I should be treated with more respect. I put up with so much at work to put food on the table for everyone. Then I come home and I have to deal with more nastiness. I do not deserve this!" thinks Jack.

In other words, Jack has his own contradicting expansion taking place. His expansion is following the same patterns as Jenna's expansion. **Sooner or later, these two contradicting expansions must collide.**

And collide they do on Thanksgiving when Jenna makes the mistake of bringing up Jack's smacking as a joke. Everyone laughs, but not Jack. He is done with this abuse. A volcanic fight erupts in front of all that are gathered. After, neither Jenna nor Jack slept that night. They were both filled with rage, an upgrade from anger. Their marriage will never be the same from this point on!

Things are out of control between Jenna and Jack since that Thanksgiving. It is like they are looking for reasons to fight, anywhere, anytime. And plenty of reasons are made available by the Law of Focus. This marriage has seen its best days. To make the long story short, Jenna and Jack soon find themselves in the divorce court fighting over the custody of the children.

How did this marriage go from smacking lips to divorce court?

When the magnetic pull of your expansion reaches a tipping point, you are no longer in control. The magnetic pull will take a life of its own and you will have to live with the consequences.

This was just one very simplified example of how the Law of Focus impacts relationships. The Law of Focus impacts all aspects of everyone's lives. It is the formula by which all that is, operates.

What happens in your life is a result of what you have focused on.
What happens in your city is a result of the collective focus of everyone regarding your city.
What happens in your state is a result of the collective focus of everyone regarding your state.
What happens in your country is a result of the collective focus of everyone regarding your country.
What happens in your world is a result of the collective focus of everyone regarding your world.

And so on...

Who designed the world to operate in this way? The Law of Focus sounds like the dumbest law ever!

Incorrect. It is the most incredible and flawless law ever! **Maybe you just did not get the user manual to teach you how to use it to your advantage.** No worries, you are now reading the manual. Whether you want peace or prosperity, it is all within your reach now.

Imagine what you can achieve if you master the art of focus?

You can achieve everything you have ever wanted! No exceptions.

The next chapter is especially important. But, before we go any further, I would like you to sit quietly today and ponder something. Take 15 minutes or more to recall major events in your life and decode how the Law of Focus played part in those events. You may not be able to decode all events of your life at this stage, because you do not know all aspects of the Law of Focus yet, but you certainly will see that many events in your life were a direct result of how you and the people around you focused collectively.

6

Bells and Whistles

"Look up and find a falling water drop and try to catch it in your palm. It takes a few seconds for it to come down...and it is a challenge to catch it, but it is so much fun." I said this to my wife to convince her to play my silly game directly under the monolithic Natural Bridge. We made it to the Natural Bridge Historic Hotel and were pleasantly surprised by the adventures that awaited us. The elderly UNI agent was correct. Getting here was easy due to the empty roads because of the pandemic. The Natural Bridge Historic Hotel is situated perfectly. You can walk to the Natural Bridge State Park from the hotel, using a tunnel. You begin your walk down to the bridge, parallel to the Cascade Creek, and you are sure to pass the remains of the oldest and the largest Arbor Vitae tree.

> **"Vires-Acquirit-Eundo" Ancient Arbor Vitae**
>
> Before dying in 1980, this more than 1600 year old specimen of the Arbor Vitae tree was the oldest and largest known in the world. It's diameter measures 56 inches. Depending on climatic conditions that determine it's growth rate, the arbor vitae increases in diameter about one inch every thirty years. Native Americans use the foliage as a source of Vitamin C to prevent scurvey.
>
> Looking back up Cascade Creek, you may see the beautifully exposed tufa deposits, tan and buff colored deposits of calcium carbonate. Layers of the same type of limestone and dolomites that form the bridge can also be seen along the trail and in the creek. The limestone is a blue-grey color.
>
> *"[Natural Bridge is] the Bridge not made by hands, that spans a river, carries a highway, and makes two mountains one."*
> — Henry Clay, American Statesman, 1777-1852

As you continue towards the Natural Bridge, it eventually emerges in the distance. We were not impressed by the Natural Bridge at first because we did not realize the sheer size of this behemoth from far away. But, as we got closer, our jaws dropped in amazement. Standing directly underneath the bridge and looking up is an experience worth having. And if you are playful like us, you would enjoy catching water drops falling from the bridge.

Image courtesy of Wikipedia

Natural Bridge has enormous proportions. Man only first discovered Natural Bridge a few hundred years ago. Nature, however, patiently worked for millions of years, with the magnificent skill to construct this monument which would stand for millennia. The arch is composed of solid grey limestone. It is 215 feet high (55 feet higher than Niagara

Falls) 40 feet thick, 100 feet wide and spans 90 feet between massive walls. The rocks that compose the bridge are early Ordovician, about 500 million years old. At its highest point, the bridge is approximately 1160 feet above sea level. This was Nature's working material. Her tool, Cedar Creek. A simple mountain stream flowing towards the sea. With these, Nature achieves her miracle. She painted her masterpiece with dull red and ochre, soft shades of yellow and cream, delicate tracings of blueish grey. According to legend, in 1750, the youthful George Washington, engaged by Lord Fairfax, proprietor of the Northern Neck of Virginia, surveyed the surrounding acreage of the Natural Bridge. During his visit, he scaled some 23 feet up the left wall of the bridge and carved his initials 'G.W.', which may still be seen today. From the literary classic, Moby Dick, to such paintings as The Peaceable Kingdom, Natural Bridge has been used to portray the ultimate natural wonder. Edward Hicks, one of America's foremost folk artists, used the Natural Bridge in his oil painting of about 1825-30. Among many famous artists to paint or sketch an image of the bridge was Frederick Edwin Church of the Hudson River School, who came to paint the bridge in 1852. He was also followed by David Johnson in 1860, a second-generation Hudson River School artist.

> *"{Natural Bridge} is something like being in a church. It almost brings tears to your eyes."*
> -Dr. Norman Vincent Peale

I love visiting natural sites like these. They remind me of the abundant beauty of our planet. They also remind me to put things in perspective. The planet has been around for 4.5 billion years. It has seen many species come and go. The dinosaurs roamed the Earth 65 million years ago and were wiped out completely, after having dominated the planet for over 165 million years. Modern humans have been around for only 200,000 years. Modern humans are the new babies of the planet. Yes, we are the newbies by comparison, but there is something so special about us. **We are equipped with tremendous creative power and bells and whistles to guide our creation unlike any of the species before us.**

What bells and whistles?

Have you ever driven one of these new vehicles that are equipped with Rear Crash-Prevention Technology (RCPT)? These vehicles are equipped with rearview cameras, rear parking sensors, and rear automatic emergency braking. I love having fun with this technology. Once, I put a trashcan behind the vehicle and tried to back into it. As I got closer, the vehicle started beeping. The closer I got, the louder and faster it beeped. I ignored the audible/visual warnings and kept going, and it engaged the breaks automatically to prevent a crash. That was awesome!

Wouldn't it be nice if our bodies were equipped with useful safety features like that?

They already are! The UNI Communications System (UCS) integrated within your body, has tons of safety features with bells and whistles. These bells and whistles have been firing your entire life, to prevent you from making mistakes and ensure you have only the best experiences. Perhaps you do not know how to recognize them, because no one has ever taught you how to recognize them.

Every time you focus on something, UCS notifies you whether it is good for you or not.
Every time you think a thought, UCS notifies you whether it is good for you or not.
Every time you make a decision, UCS notifies you whether it is good for you or not.

Every time you take an action, UCS notifies you whether it is good for you or not.

And so on...

The UCS always gives you real-time feedback to let you know whether, whatever you are up to, is good for you or not. Perhaps you have not known about these bells and whistles until now. No worries, it all ends here, today. By the end of this chapter, you will know all you need to know about the safety features of your body. Please allow me to educate you on the UCS by analyzing the incidents between our favorite couple Jenna and Jack, and how Jenna could have saved her marriage if she had listened to the bells and whistles of her UCS.

The UCS system is always turned on, active, and monitoring. When Jenna's ears first registered Jack's smacking lips and she focused on it, UCS became alert. Jenna's eyes were the next to focus on Jack's smacking. The UCS was still alert and monitoring what Jenna was up to. Jenna then decided to have negative thoughts regarding Jack's smacking.

"Why is he chewing like a pig? Does he not know manners? Was he raised in a barn?"

The moment those negative thoughts took place in Jenna's head, is the exact moment UCS knew that Jenna had taken her first step in the wrong direction and something had to be done to correct it.

Do you remember that a new pattern of neurons started to fire in Jenna's brain for the first time as she thought those negative thoughts?

If Jenna continued to repeat those negative thoughts, that pattern will soon solidify into a negative neural pathway. Repetition of negative thoughts creates a negative neural pathway. Having a negative neural pathway makes it easier to repeat negative thoughts and repeating negative thoughts continues to strengthen the negative neural pathway. **The stronger the neural pathway, the stronger the magnetic pull.**

Do you see how vicious cycles are created?

The UCS knew that it will be harmful to the well-being of Jenna's marriage if the neural pathway solidified. Therefore, to save Jenna from making this mistake, the UCS intervened immediately by ringing the first warning bell. The UCS decided to induce the emotion of "annoyance" in Jenna's body; to interrupt her thought pattern, and to jolt her out of thinking those negative thoughts.

If you are sitting peacefully pondering something and a mosquito bites you, inducing toxin in your body, wouldn't that interrupt your thoughts?

It is the same reason why the UCS induced "annoyance" in Jenna's body which is a mild toxin like a mosquito-bite. Jenna recognized the emotion of annoyance but did not know that she was supposed to stop and revise her thoughts, until they felt good, to undo the damage from her negative thoughts about Jack's smacking. No one had ever taught Jenna how the UCS worked. In other words, Jenna was like a deaf and blind driver, in a vehicle equipped with RCPT! So, the first warning bell from the UCS went unnoticed by Jenna. **If Jenna had recognized this warning bell and revised her thoughts about Jack's smacking until they felt good or focus away from Jack's smacking, and on to something else that felt good; she would have saved her marriage. The correct time to act is when you notice the very first UCS warning bell.**

Instead, Jenna continued her focus on the smacking and the Law of Focus expanded her annoyance by bringing nose hair to her attention. As Jenna thought additional negative thoughts about the nose hair, the UCS took more drastic measures to jolt her out of thinking those negative thoughts.

If you are sitting peacefully, pondering something and a bee, stings you, inducing more toxin than a mosquito-bite, wouldn't that interrupt your thoughts?

It is the same reason why the UCS upgraded annoyance to irritation which is more toxic to the body. But our deaf and blind driver Jenna is still unaware of the warning bells. She assumes that her irritation is a natural response to Jack's behavior, and she is not doing anything wrong.

What did Jenna do next?

She met with her BFF for a good old-fashioned husband bashing. By the end of that dinner with the BFF, the UCS had upgraded Jenna's irritation to anger.

If you are sitting peacefully, pondering something, and a scorpion stings you, inducing more toxin than a bee-sting, wouldn't that interrupt your thoughts?

It is the same reason why the UCS upgraded irritation to anger which is a lot more toxic to the body. As you know already, Jenna does recognize that she is angry but assumes it is a natural response to Jack's behavior, and she is not doing anything wrong.

As you are aware, after the Thanksgiving blowout, both Jenna and Jack had upgraded to rage.

Of course, all the UCS warning bells had gone unnoticed because **Jenna, just like all other misguided humans, thinks that the presence of negative emotions is a normal reaction to something that someone else is doing wrong.** She could not be more wrong. **The presence of negative emotions is a clear warning from the UCS that you, YES YOU, are** thinking thoughts that will harm you unless you stop, and revise your thoughts until they feel better or focus away from the cause of the negative thoughts.

That last sentence holds the key to creating a life of your choosing! This is also a good time to explain what is happening with the magnetic pull of the expansion as Jenna managed to upgrade her negative emotion from annoyance to rage. When Jenna was annoyed, the magnetic pull of the expansion was like pulling a kayak, towards a dock called "Jenna's marriage". A kayak colliding with a dock is not a big issue. When Jenna reached irritation, the magnetic pull of the expansion was like pulling a jet ski, towards the dock. A jet ski colliding with the dock will do some damage, but still recoverable. Reaching anger, was like pulling a boat towards the dock but reaching rage was like pulling a mighty Naval Destroyer, straight towards the little dock called "Jenna's marriage". It will tear through the dock effortlessly and there won't be anything left to recover.

Luckily, Jenna can always re-marry and start over.

Sure, but what about her well-defined neural pathways and the magnetic pull of the expansion from her first marriage?

They are both sitting around the corner with a baseball bat, just waiting for Jenna to turn the corner again in her second marriage. And when she does, BAM! There goes the second marriage, and the vicious cycle continues. This is why, people that have been in troubled relationships, keep attracting the same type of relationships unless they take measures to stop the vicious cycle once and for all.

You will learn how to stop such cycles in this book.

Needless to say, every time you ignore a UCS warning bell, there is a price to pay. The magnetic pull becomes stronger and stronger every time you ignore a UCS warning bell. **When the magnetic pull of your expansion reaches a tipping point, you are no longer in control. The magnetic pull will take a life of its own and you will have to live with the consequences.** In Jenna's example, she could have recovered when the pull was the size of a kayak, jet ski, or boat. Once the pull reached the destroyer size, it was over. Jenna and Jack were no longer in control to stop it. At that point, the fights between the two of them would become automated. Anything can start a fight anywhere, anytime.

Have you seen shameless couples that fight anywhere, anytime, regardless of how ridiculous they appear to others?

They have reached the tipping point. They are no longer in control. The destroyer-size magnetic pull is running the show and they are just the puppets of the pull. We all have various amounts of pull regarding all topics in our lives. Whether it is relationship, health, wealth, politics, religion, or anything else. We have pull regarding everything we have observed and focused on since our birth and even before. The good news is the pull is not always negative. On some topics, we have a positive pull, on some it is neutral and for the rest, it is negative. For the topics where you have a positive pull, the results are amazing. These are the topics where you get to experience the true genius behind the Law of Focus. Once you have a positive pull going, everything seems to work out and things fall in place for you. It keeps getting better and better and there is no end to it. It is easy to live a blissful life once you figure out how to expand the positive pull.

It is easy to experience peace once you have expanded the positive pull of peace.

It is easy to experience health once you have expanded the positive pull of health.

It is easy to experience wealth once you have expanded the positive pull of wealth.

It is easy to experience happiness once you have expanded the positive pull of happiness.

And so on...

Can you see how the political upheaval of the last few years in America has created so much negative pull, in two opposite directions?

Can you see how these opposing pulls are now colliding and giving birth to so much chaos?

Can you see how all the focus on the pandemic has generated so much negative pull that it shut down the planet, toyed with the economy, and has created unparalleled misery in the world?

Can you count the number of warning bells fired by your UCS, regarding your focus on the pandemic matters, that you may have ignored just like Jenna?

Once you finish reading this very important chapter, I would like you to ponder something. Let us identify the type and size of your pull regarding some of the most common topics in your life. To create a baseline, download this tracking sheet: http://bit.ly/mybaseline

Do not be limited to the topics on the tracking sheet. Some topics such as "Spouse" will have many sub-topics such as "in-laws", "spouse's friends", etc. Feel free to add all other topics that are important to you on the tracking sheet. Then, identify whether you have a positive pull or negative pull regarding each topic.

How do I do that?

Engage your UCS, young Jedi! The UCS already knows where you are on every topic. I understand this might be your first time consciously engaging the UCS and you may not get a good reading, but there is nothing to lose. All you have to do is focus on the subject and let your thoughts flow. **If your thoughts generate positive emotions or feel good, you have a positive pull. If your thoughts generate negative emotions or feel bad, you have a negative pull.** On some topics, you may get a neutral reading which is also acceptable. Write down the type of pull you have next to each topic.

Now let us rate each topic for the size of the pull. Let us use the scale of a kayak, jet ski, boat, and destroyer.

How would I know the size of the pull?

The UCS got you covered again.

First, recall the intensity of your emotions related to each topic. The more intense the emotion, the bigger the pull.

Second, recall the speed and automation of your thoughts. If your thoughts took off like a wild banshee and kept coming at a rapid speed in an automated fashion, to the point where the thoughts started thinking themselves, you are more towards the destroyer side.

This exercise will establish your baseline and will allow you to track your progress as you learn how to eliminate the negative pull and increase the positive pull on all topics.

Note: *Once this book is published, I plan to develop an official workbook and other material that will help you master the teachings herein. All material would be made available on Amazon.com. Feel free to search the keywords "Pandemic to Peace Official" and see what is available at the time of your reading of this book.*

* * *

After relaxing under the natural bridge for a while, we continued forward on the Cedar Creek Trail. We soon reached a reconstructive archeology project of a Monacan Indian village. The village depicts glimpses of what life would have been like in a small Monacan Village 300 years ago along the banks of Cedar Creek.

We are very thankful that every site we visit during the pandemic, is very quiet. Occasionally, we will see another tourist or two. It feels like we are among very few humans left in the world and the rest of the world has just disappeared.

We continued further on the trail and found a Saltpeter Cave and learned about how it took 18 bushels of soak and 10 bushels of elm ashes to make 100 pounds of good saltpeter.

It seems like the UNI setup a surprise at every corner of this easy hiking trail.

We continued eagerly and discover the lost river.

Legend has it that, in later years, several unsuccessful attempts were made to locate the underground channels of the Lost River. Colored dyes and flotation devices of all types have failed to determine the source and destination of this mysterious subterranean river.

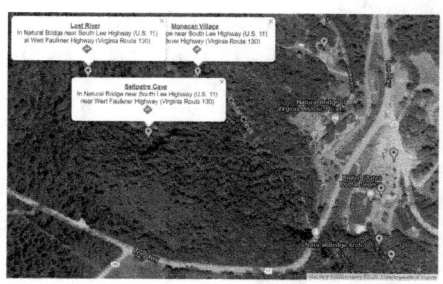

Image courtesy of Google and Commonwealth of Virginia

We walked just a little further and the sounds of a waterfall registered on our ears. We picked up our pace and soon arrived to witness the soothing sounds of the Lace Waterfall.

Image courtesy of landreport.com

We closed our eyes and listened to the soothing sounds of the waterfall to our heart's content! While our bodies and minds were zoned out, we still maintained **awareness**.

7

Awareness

You must become more aware of your UCS warning bells from this point forward. **This is a practice that must continue for the rest of your life.** If you felt **inspired** while reading the last statement, you are on the fast track and you will soon enjoy the countless benefits of working with the UNI. If the last statement felt like work, that is your UCS warning bell indicating that your thoughts regarding the last statement are incorrect.

See how easy it is to be aware of your UCS?

Please memorize the following list of emotions.

Fab-5 : (Joy/Appreciation/Empowerment/Freedom/Love)

The list above represents the best life-enhancing emotions you can have. I call them the "Fab-5" (5 Fabulous Emotions). Also, memorize the list below:

Fan-14 : (Joy/Appreciation/Empowerment/Freedom/Love, Passion,

Enthusiasm/Eagerness/Happiness, Positive Expectation/Belief, Optimism, Hopefulness, Contentment)

That is a list of good emotions. I call them the "Fan-14" (14 Fantastic Emotions). The emotions are listed in the order of priority. That means Joy, Appreciation, Empowerment, Freedom, and Love are the best life-enhancing emotions you can have. While you are capable of experiencing a wide range of emotions, the emotions not included in the list above are life-eroding to a varying degree. If the emotion you are feeling at any given point, is a Fan-14, you are enhancing your life. If the emotion you are feeling at any given point is not a Fan-14, you are experiencing a UCS warning bell and eroding your life. Enhancing your life means everything you have ever wanted in terms of health, wealth, and happiness (and more) is on its way to you. Eroding your life means everything bad that you think can happen to you (and more), is on its way to you.

Earlier in the book, you learned that Jenna's UCS induced negative emotions in her to jolt her out of thinking negative thoughts. The UCS did that to stop Jenna from walking down the path of suffering. Negative emotions are only meant to be temporary warning bells. It is not good for you to dwell on negative emotions for longer periods. **As soon as you catch yourself feeling a negative emotion, you are supposed to stop and correct your focus.** This is the process that must be followed if you wish to work with the UNI and create a life of your choosing. Correcting your focus generally requires correcting your thoughts, but not always. Sometimes, it requires turning your eyes away from looking at something disturbing or turning your nose away from smelling something disturbing, or turning one or more of your senses away from something disturbing. **Correcting your focus requires turning one or more parts of your being away from the cause of the disturbance and refocusing them differently until you feel one of the Fan-14.**

Your UCS is like the RCPT of a vehicle. The Vehicle equipped with

RCPT beeps louder and louder as you get closer and closer to a crash. Just like that, your UCS beeps louder and louder by upgrading to worse feeling emotions as you get closer and closer to a disastrous event in your life. The loudest UCS warning bells are the emotions of Revenge, Hatred, Rage, Jealousy, Fear, Grief, Desperation, Despair, or Powerlessness. I call them the Nasty-9.

Nasty-9 : (Revenge, Hatred, Rage, Jealousy, Fear, Grief, Desperation, Despair, or Powerlessness)

When two people get into a violent conflict, do you think they were experiencing Joy, Appreciation, Empowerment, Freedom, or Love during that conflict?

Of course not. They were experiencing one or more of the Nasty-9. All acts of violence have taken place from the Nasty-9. The video of George Floyd's death is one of the most viral videos of our times. We all know the chaos that ensued George's death. You have likely watched the video of this event already. Let us apply what we have learned so far to that event.

While George was pinned down under the officers was he feeling Joy, Appreciation, Empowerment, Freedom, or Love at that moment?

I think not. It is safe to say he was probably experiencing one of the Nasty-9 like Fear, Desperation, Despair, or Powerlessness.

Do you think the officers were feeling Joy, Appreciation, Empowerment, Freedom, or Love at that moment?

I think not. It is safe to say they were also experiencing one of the Nasty-9 or something very close to it.

We all know how that encounter between George and the officers ended and the chaos and suffering that followed.

Wouldn't the world be a better place without such chaos and suffering?

So, let us make an effort to make this world a better place. It starts with you learning to be aware of your UCS and what it is telling you. **It is never too late to master the UCS.** All that is required is consistent practice. You will now learn how to train yourself to become aware of your UCS.

Use your cell phone and set up a recurring reminder for every 15 minutes. Set the sound of that reminder to something soothing, gentle, or natural. For example, I used a dewdrop sound when I was learning, which felt like a drop of water falling. Your phone probably has a library of tones to choose from. Choose the tone that feels the best to your ears. Set the text of this reminder to ask "How am I feeling?"

This reminder will go off every 15 minutes during your day and ask how you are feeling. Every time it goes off, here is what you have to do:

- Take a few moments to observe how you are feeling.
- If you are not feeling one of the Fan-14, take a few deep breaths and make a deliberate effort to refocus until you are feeling one of the Fan-14 emotions.
- Do whatever is necessary to refocus such as correcting your breathing and posture, stretching, taking a walk, listening to good music. Figure out a list of things that make you feel Fan-14 and perform what is on the list until you feel a Fan-14.
- The process of training your mind to refocus is the same as going to the gym regularly to build muscles. Just like exercising, training your mind to refocus will be very difficult in the beginning, but will become easier and more automated with practice. **Persis-**

tent practice is the key to success when it comes to training your mind.

When you first begin your training, it is not likely that you will catch yourself experiencing one of the Nasty-9. This is because the Nasty-9 comes with a destroyer-size negative pull. And because of that pull, if you are experiencing a Nasty-9 and your reminder goes off, you will most likely not even hear the reminder. Even if you hear it, you will most likely be unable to refocus and dissolve the Nasty-9. The ultimate goal is to be able to dissolve the Nasty-9 but it is very difficult at the beginning of your training. So, I will offer you something else for the Nasty-9, while you take baby steps towards mastering your UCS.

Previously, you created a baseline of your pull regarding various topics. Review that baseline and identify the topics where you have a destroyer-size negative pull. Now swear to avoid focusing on those topics. Just walk away from those topics. If your friend is one of those topics, end that friendship. If your boss is one of those topics, find another job.

What if your spouse is one of those topics?

I understand it is not practical to eliminate all topics that evoke the Nasty-9 from you. **At least not right away. But you must vow to eliminate those topics one by one from your life. Start with the easiest one and then progress forward. It does not matter how long it takes to eliminate them. Just do it with patience, even if it takes decades to eliminate them all.** For the remaining topics on your list, you will be able to avoid reaching the destroyer-size negative pull using the exercises included later in the book.

For any topics where you have negative pull, I would suggest trying the Thought Field Therapy (TFT) developed by American psychologist, Dr. Roger Callahan. Here is an excerpt from www.tfttapping.com:

"Thought Field Therapy (TFT) provides a code to nature's healing system. When applied to problems, TFT solves the fundamental causes, balancing the body's energy system and eliminates most negative emotions... within minutes.

Dr. Roger Callahan, our founder, achieved worldwide recognition, acceptance, and use of Thought Field Therapy. We believe we can have a significant impact on the decrease of human suffering if everyone has these tools at their disposal.

TFT tapping is brief, effective psychotherapy for the rapid and natural healing of negative emotions and psychological problems. Thought Field Therapy uses nature's therapeutic system to balance the body's energy system promoting natural healing and improved mental health."

The aforementioned website provides training and information on Thought Field Therapy. Finding a TFT therapist and getting a session used to be difficult and expensive but not anymore. Thanks to YouTube, you can find TFT videos for any particular emotion, trauma, or phobia. Simply search for terms such as "TFT for anger", "TFT for anxiety" or "TFT for spider phobia" and you will find the exact TFT sequence. **Try the sequence while you are feeling the negative emotion or phobia.** While TFT is considered pseudoscience, many people claim it permanently eliminates phobias and negative emotions associated with certain topics. In other words, it can eliminate negative pull associated with topics where you have negative pull. You may need multiple sessions depending on the size of the pull. Try it and see if it works for you.

The reason for being aware of your UCS is simple. When your nose registers a foul smell, you automatically make the effort to move away from it to avoid getting sick. Your nose is one of your senses designed to prevent you from getting sick from foul smells. Just like that, your UCS is also one of your senses, designed to prevent bad experiences and disasters in your life. When you become aware of emotions that are not Fan-14, move away from them as quickly as possible.

Once you reach that point, the magic of life will unfold! And you will not need cell phone reminders anymore.

It is normal to have some negative emotions and you can even create positive outcomes from negative emotions. If you did not feel hunger you wouldn't know when your body required nutrition to stay alive. Just like that, **without negative emotions, you wouldn't know what is standing in your way to your dream life.** It is not your goal to eliminate all negative emotions from your life, it is your goal to quickly become aware of them and refocus. If you master your UCS you can quickly identify and eliminate the roadblocks from your health, wealth, and happiness.

How would you perform this exercise if you do not have a cell phone?

Easy. Review your environment and identify an object that you observe frequently such as a light bulb or a tree or anything made of plastic. Every time you see that object, pause, and perform the exercise as if it were a cell phone reminder. There are many other ways to set such reminders without requiring a cell phone. Just be creative and you will see many alternatives in your environment. Some of you may become numb to hearing the cell reminders after a while. If that happens, change the tone of the reminder or come up with an alternative reminder in your environment.

* * *

We slept well at the Natural Bridge Historic Hotel and continued to enjoy our road trip together. We reveled in how much fun we were having and how this trip is so affordable compared to past vacations we have taken. Fun, just like everything else, has nothing to do with the amount of money you spend. It has everything to do with your focus. In other words, fun is all about letting your UCS guide you to the experiences that will give you that feeling of fun!

We stopped at the Caverns at Natural Bridge, minutes away from the hotel, which was especially exciting because I have never seen caverns in person before. While the Caverns at Natural Bridge are not the biggest, they are a wonderful sight for a first-timer. We were so excited as we approached the entrance and then we saw the sign: "Masks are required to enter."

"It is annoying to wear a mask on a hot summer day. I'll have to walk back to the vehicle to get them. We are perfectly healthy, and they shouldn't force us to wear one." I thought.

As these thoughts popped into my head, my UCS fired a warning bell, and I felt a bit of frustration and irritation. I knew that my negative thoughts had caused the UCS to fire this warning. Therefore, my thoughts must be incorrect, and I have two options:

- correct my thoughts until I feel a Fan-14
- focus on something else that evokes a Fan-14

I looked around but did not see anything that would evoke a Fan-14. So, I selected the first option and I deliberately corrected my thoughts.

"The vehicle is only 20 feet away. Why am I even complaining about having to walk back? We are going into a cave; I do not know what the air would be like down there. It is probably safer to have a mask on anyway." I practiced those thoughts while walking back to the vehicle. And then I saw another sign which stated,

"It is always 54-degree Fahrenheit inside the caverns."

I could not help but chuckle! Just a moment ago I was whining about heaving to wear a mask on a hot day when it is actually going to be cold inside the caverns. **I chuckled because the UCS does not miss a thing -- ever! The UCS already knew it would be cold inside the caverns and wearing summer clothes or complaining about the masks was not in our best interest. So, the UCS corrected everything in one shot by making me aware of the sign on my way to the vehicle where we kept both masks and warm clothes. Once you master the UCS, you avoid the potholes of life and everything flows flawlessly.**

As I emerged into the depths of the caverns, I was blown away by the sheer size of the chambers surrounding me.

It was very interesting to see an underground stream passing through the caverns, hundreds of feet below ground.

While we were in the deepest cavern, the tour guide asked everyone to silence and put away our cell phones. He then turned off the lights. It instantly became pitch black. I could not even see my own hands. We all took a few moments and observed the silence. Here we were, in the belly of the beast, almost 35 stories underground, left with nothing but our thoughts. All my senses had just vanished, and I was left with only one thought...

*"How awesome would it be to **meditate** in a cave?"*

8

Meditation

"Take a look at the clock and you will realize that almost an hour has passed since you started your trance. However, you may feel like you were in a trance for just a few minutes," said The Amazing Kreskin, pointing towards the clock on the wall, inside a closed-door training room.

"What did he do to me? What just happened to my body? Was I drugged? Why am I buzzing? Where did all the fatigue go? What is happening to me?" So many questions sprung in my head as I looked at the clock in disbelief, still trying to cope with what had just transpired in that closed-door training room. I did not have the answers, but I knew that I had experienced something unique and very powerful. I knew that my life would never be the same from that point on.

It all started very early in the morning. I had been introduced to the UNI recently and I was learning how to work with the UNI. My life was changing rapidly ever since I started working with them. They had arranged for me to meet The Amazing Kreskin and learn the power of my mind, meditation, hypnosis, subconscious programming and so much more. I was meeting Kreskin in New York City early that morning. I had to wake up even earlier, get ready, drive from Princeton, NJ to NYC, find parking in NYC, and be in the room to learn from Kreskin. This was around the year 2010 and many of you can understand how frustrating it is to find parking in NYC. Just the anxiety around the whole trip kept me awake the night before. I did not sleep well, and I was already tired when I woke up. I had given up caffeine recently as part of my commitment to health. So, I dragged my sluggish self, kicking and screaming to NYC and barely made it in time.

"This Kreskin better be worth the hassle." I thought as I slumped in the chair waiting for him. For those that do not know The Amazing Kreskin, here is an excerpt from his website: https://bit.ly/3j2DIdB

With a showman's flair, a comedian's wit, and the capacities of a bona fide Mentalist or thought reader, The Amazing Kreskin has, for six decades, dramatized the unique facets of the human mind...his own. His very name has become an integral part of pop culture throughout the world.

During the past fifty years, Kreskin has had a television series, his own board game by Milton Bradley, twenty published books, and a major motion picture inspired by his work.

In the 1970s Kreskin headlined his own television series for five and a half seasons called, 'The Amazing World of Kreskin' which can now be viewed on www.hulu.com. The airline industry estimates that Kreskin has flown over 3 million miles, to reach a vast international audience with his unique brand of Mentalism.

To reveal his remarkable diversity, John Romero, a leading gaming authority quotes in his book, 'Las Vegas The Untold Story' "Kreskin is the most dangerous person in the world with a deck of cards. The casinos would rather deal to Willie Sutton".

Actor/Producer Tom Hanks released in 2009 the feature film, 'The Great Buck Howard". It is announced at the end of the movie that the inspiration for the main character is The Amazing Kreskin. That character is played by the star of the movie, John Malkovich.

In the 2010 movie, 'Dinner for Schmucks', the character played by Zach Galifianakis has as his hero and influence, The Amazing Kreskin, which further exemplifies the wide scope of Kreskin's exposure and attention. It is showcased with his recurring appearances on Johnny Carson, Regis Philbin, David Letterman, and most recently Jimmy Fallon, Neil Cavuto, and Howard Stern.

2014 brought a whole new realm to Kreskin's arsenal when he mentally trained three up and coming boxers to victory. One of the winners was Heather "The Heat" Hardy and he was further brought in to prepare and condition her mentally for a contest of worldwide dimension. In October of 2014, he was brought into the ring to join her in the celebration of her success; a success that he helped prepare her for in the preceding months. She had just won the WBC International Junior Featherweight Championship of the World.

Through the years Kreskin has received worldwide recognition for extraordinary predictions, often dealing with international affairs, and sports. On Late Night with Jimmy Fallon, Kreskin predicted the 2012 United States Presidential Election, 18 months before Election Day. As revealed on Fox television for the 2016 Super Bowl, Kreskin made three predictions. He foresaw the deciding quarter of the game, the winning team, and their final score.

In March 2016 Kreskin released his 20th book entitled, "In Real Time" featuring his major predictions for the next several hundred years. The day after Donald Trump was elected to the Presidency, Fox Television News revealed that Kreskin predicted Trump's election 11 months ahead of time, Live on December 9th, 2015 on FOX 5 Good Day DC Show in Washington, D.C.

Kreskin now offers the sum of 1 Million dollars to anyone who can prove

that he employs paid secret assistants, or confederates, or utilizes hidden, secret, electronic devices to accomplish his mental presentations.

At 83 years of age, Kreskin shows no signs of slowing down. He continues to perform his legendary live shows in front of packed audiences around the world, playing over 200+ dates yearly.

Needless to say, The Amazing Kreskin works with the UNI. My jaw was pretty much on the floor the entire time as The Amazing Kreskin demonstrated his mental abilities in that closed-door training room. Here I was, an accomplished, world-traveling, well-paid, proud CEO, and I thought I knew things but I really did not know much about how my own mind worked. The cherry on the top that day, was when The Amazing Kreskin put me in a relaxing hypnotic trance while I was sitting in my chair. Hypnotic Trance is a form of guided meditation with the addition of beneficial suggestions. It was the most amazing relaxation I had ever experienced. It felt like five minutes of relaxation but almost an hour had passed according to the clock on the wall. I was not asleep during that time. I was aware of my surroundings but still in a very deep state of relaxation. When I came out of it, my body buzzed for hours and felt as light as a feather. All of my fatigue had vanished as if I had gotten a solid night of slumber. In fact, it was even better than that. I felt as if my brain and mind had been washed and rebooted for the first time in my life! I grew up in India where meditation originated and is a common practice even today, but this was truly my first time experiencing it. Ever since that day, meditation has become a regular practice in my life, and it will be that for the rest of my life. Meditation is a requirement to work with the UNI.

Meditation is the most powerful tool available to mankind and this priceless tool is FREE!

If I have to name 10 benefits of meditation, I can.
If I have to name 100 benefits of meditation, I can.

If I have to name 1,000 benefits of meditation, I can.

But it is my goal to keep this book as short as possible. It is not necessary to learn everything about meditation to benefit from it. Therefore, I will refer you to other articles and amazing books as appropriate if you are curious. For a summary of different types of meditation, refer to these articles:
https://bit.ly/319QIrQ
https://bit.ly/2Iva8Rf

Also, review the 150 benefits of meditation to see how it can help you:
https://bit.ly/3nPyS7b

I will now set you up with an easy and free meditation program. Every brain is wired differently and therefore, different types of meditation resonate with different people. I prefer body scan meditations. Explore these free sites with downloadable meditations:
https://bit.ly/33XIyV9
https://bit.ly/2SW6dyV
https://bit.ly/379Gone

You can also sample additional meditations on YouTube or apps such as Let us Meditate, Calm, or Headspace until you find what resonates with you. My absolute favorite app is called Synctuition (https://bit.ly/3dtscXq) They use advanced audio techniques such as personalized frequency, rhythmic entertainment, binaural beats, gamma waves, and 3D sound effects to create an incredible relaxation experience. I use it before sleep to wind down and it is a treat for the mind. It is not free, but they do have a free trial. Try it out and if you can afford it, buy it. It comes with a carefully organized library which I have found to be very useful. Winding down with meditation before sleep is powerful and gives you significantly better sleep. Here are some pro-tips you can follow to enhance your meditation experience:

- Select a quiet environment where you will not be disturbed for the duration of your meditation. This is only required when you are new to meditation. Once you have some experience with meditation, you can meditate anywhere, anytime for as long or as short as you want.
- Ideally, you should meditate 3 times a day. When you wake up, after lunch, and before sleep. Pick the times that work the best for you.
- Experiment with the times, length, and types of meditations until you find what works the best for your brain. I generally rotate among different types when I feel **inspired** to do so.
- Once in a while, you may be able to reach a deep relaxation state when you zone out for what feels like a short/long time. During this zoned-out state, your brain and mind get a much-needed reboot. You will know when this happens because you will feel more refreshed than ever before in your life. I do not get to this state with every meditation but when I am really tired, it seems to happen more consistently than when I am not tired. Whether you get to this state or not, meditation still helps you in unbelievable ways.
- Meditation can unlock superhuman abilities for some people depending on the brain's wiring and genetic makeup. From telepathy to telekinesis, self-healing to lucid dreaming, astral projection to acute awareness, the possibilities are endless. Most meditators will see some increase in their abilities even if they do not attain superhuman abilities.

This chapter would not be complete until I emphasize one of the main reasons why meditation is a requirement to work with the UNI. That reason is intuition/inspiration. **Meditation enhances your ability to recognize your intuitions and follow-through on your inspirations.**

9

Co-creation

This is an important chapter.

Your social media apps upload your data to the social media platform in the cloud using your internet connection. The social media platform then analyzes that data to understand you better. Just like that, the UCS, installed in every living being, collects and uploads all data to the UNI. The UCS uploads everything including the state of your body down to the cellular level, your thoughts, your intentions, your desires, and everything else. This data collection is unbelievably massive, but the UNI systems are advanced enough to instantaneously process all data, from all living beings. The UNI will never misuse this data. All information is used only to enhance your life, **according to your instructions,** and to prevent you from making life-eroding mistakes. **The UNI uses this data to coordinate people, circumstances, events, and more to create the life of your choosing.** For example, if you are focused on something boring, your posture would slump, and your breathing would slow down which will result in a lack of oxygen to your vital organs. Your vital organs not getting oxygen is a problem that must be solved. The UCS will upload this data to the UNI. The

UNI systems will process this data instantly and recognize that your body needs to yawn to solve the problem. The act of yawning will flood your body with oxygen and resolve the issue. The UNI will message the UCS with the solution. Your UCS will pass this information to you using its unique method. **You will receive/recognize this information as intuition.**

🔊 in·tu·i·tion
/ˌint(y)o͞oˈiSH(ə)n/

noun

the ability to understand something immediately, without the need for conscious reasoning.
"we shall allow our intuition to guide us"

Similar: instinct • intuitiveness • sixth sense • divination • clairvoyance • second sight • ESP (extrasensory perception)

Opposite: intellect

- a thing that one knows or considers likely from instinctive feeling rather than conscious reasoning.
  plural noun: **intuitions**
  "your insights and intuitions as a native speaker are positively sought"

Similar: hunch • feeling • feeling in one's bones • gut feeling • funny feeling • inkling • sneaking suspicion • suspicion • impression • premonition • presentiment • foreboding • satori • feeling in one's water

Image courtesy of Google

Intuition and inspiration work hand in hand. Some intuitions may require action from you in due time. In your example, the action of yawning is required from you rather quickly. **Therefore, UCS will escalate/upgrade the intuition to inspiration.** In other words, you will be inspired to yawn.

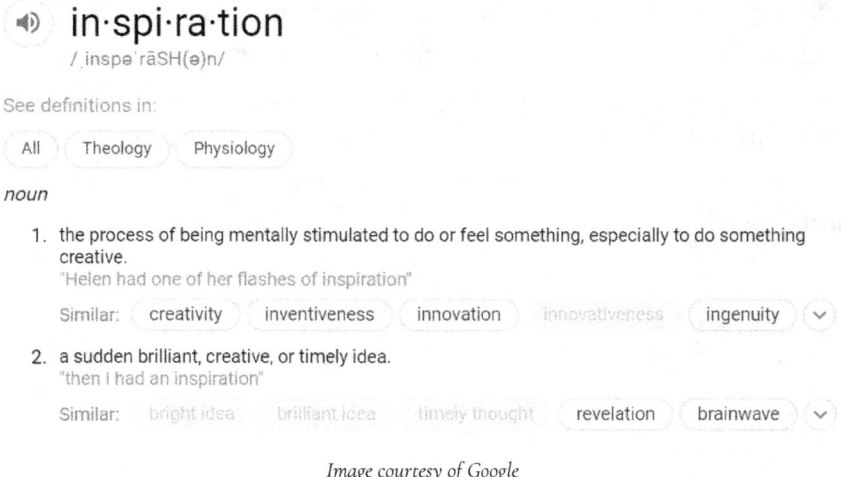

Image courtesy of Google

It is important to recognize your intuitions and follow-through on your inspirations because they are custom-designed for you, to guide you to your best life experience.

Animals in the wild recognize their intuitions and follow-through on their inspirations effortlessly. Even your domesticated pets are pretty good at doing so. For example, your dog will sometimes eat grass when it is inspired to do so. The dog may be inspired to eat grass to correct a variety of issues. These issues may include improving digestion, treating intestinal worms, or fulfilling unmet nutritional needs. When some dog owners see this, they reprimand the dog to domesticate it further. With enough scolding, the dog learns to ignore the intuition and no longer eats grass even when it is inspired to do so. Since humans are the most domesticated beings on the planet, we are the most unaware of our intuitions and we do not follow through on our inspirations. Consequently, our planet is full of writers that do not write and singers that do not sing and chefs that do not cook, and so on...

If recognizing our intuitions and following-through on our inspirations is so important, why doesn't the UNI just force us to do so?

Because it would violate your **free will**.

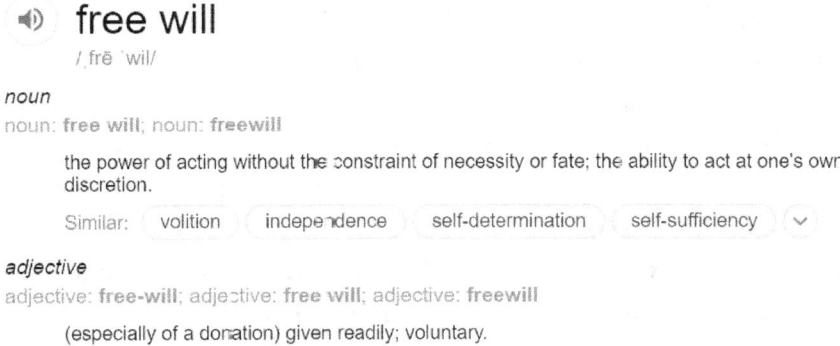

Image courtesy of Google

The UNI will always honor your free will because that was the agreement you had made with the UNI before your birth. You wanted to create your own reality on planet earth. You wanted to be the boss. So, you asked the UNI to propose solutions to your problems but let you be in charge of deciding what to do with the solutions.

I do think it would be hilarious if UNI forced the solutions upon you. That would mean...

You would burp (or worse) in the middle of your wedding vows because you were bloated, and the solution was forced upon you!

There is a pizza place near us that allows me to build my own pizza. I get to choose the crust, the sauce, toppings, and everything else. The pizza comes out delicious and perfect every time because it was made for me using my own instructions. Your life is the same way, and your free will allows you to choose what you want!

Let us put together all you have learned so far to understand how you create your own reality.

Your focus determines your creation. As soon as you focus on something, your UCS notifies you whether it is a good creation or not. The UCS is like having the training wheels on your bicycle so you will never fall. You have some time to change your focus before the Law of Focus gets involved and begins the expansion of whatever you are focused upon. This buffer allows you to correct your focus, based on the UCS feedback, if necessary. If the UCS gives you a green light regarding your focus, meaning you feel one of the Fan-14, you are clear to focus on that topic as long as you can or want. **The longer you focus on it, the faster it will expand/manifest in your life. The higher the intensity of your focus, the faster it will expand/manifest in your life.** For example, if you are alone and want a mate, thinking about how lonely you are will trigger a UCS warning bell. But, thinking about what your mate will be like and what fun things you would do together, will evoke Fan-14 from you. Let us assume you have become very good at daydreaming about your mate and you are only evoking Fan-14 when you focus on the topic of your mate. Your focus will continue to expand the positive pull of your mate until the tipping point is reached and Voila! Your mate will be introduced to you. The UNI, based on all the data it has collected from you, will identify the most suitable mate for you and coordinate everything required so the two of you can meet. I know this is a simplified example, but this is exactly how everything works! **This is called co-creation. The UNI coordinates people, circumstances, events, and more, involving all living beings as necessary to create the life of your choosing.** This book will give you everything you need to master the art of co-creation, so you can create the life of your choosing.

As you may have recognized already, I have left you some breadcrumbs throughout the book. We have reached a point in this book where I can begin to explain some of the breadcrumbs using the newfound knowledge from this chapter.

When I was sitting at Leu Gardens, the day after having witnessed the fight among my friends over their political beliefs, I was incapable of recognizing the UCS warnings. The topic of politics has reached the destroyer size negative pull in America and around the globe. Therefore, I was feeling a Nasty-9 and the UCS warnings were not enough to jolt me out of it. So, the UNI located an owl sitting on the adjacent tree and inspired it to hoot in the middle of the day. Hearing that very odd sound made me jolt out of my incorrect focus. That is co-creation. The reason I always found perfect parking in Princeton downtown, is because the UNI inspired someone parked there to pull out at the exact moment I arrived. That is co-creation. It is the same reason the CEO of the company that benefited from my business introduction, was inspired to gift me $50,000. I make business introductions all the time. The CEO did not owe me anything for that introduction. It happened that way because the UNI was aware of my $50,000 demand and the fact that the CEO had benefited tremendously from my business introduction. Therefore, inspiring the CEO to write me an unexpected check for $50,000 was the easiest way to meet my demand. That is co-creation. This is also why I was not surprised when the elderly man sitting in a rocking chair at the Big Meadows Lodge started a conversation with me and gave me precise instructions on what I should do next. The UNI inspired him to have a conversation with me because I had asked the UNI to guide me during my road trip. All living beings are UNI agents because, at one point or another, we are inspired by the UNI to act in a certain way. **Ultimately, these meaningful synchronicities show us how important it is to recognize our intuitions and follow-through on our inspirations.** When you do that, the results are incredible!

Please review some of the documented examples of phenomena called "Hysterical Strength": https://bit.ly/30PZ6ML

Hysterical strength is a display of extreme strength by humans, beyond what is believed to be normal, usually occurring when people are in life-and-death situations. Common anecdotal examples include parents lifting vehicles to rescue their children. Most parents will do anything to save their children. Therefore, when a life-threatening situation occurs with a child, and the UNI inspires the parent to perform a superhuman task to save the child, the parent performs that task without hesitation, **the UNI supplies the necessary strength,** and lives are saved!

Incredible!

Do you remember the George Floyd video?
Have you seen both, the video from a bystander and the bodycam of one of the officers?
Did you notice that several bystanders showed up at the scene and pleaded multiple times to the officers to release George?

These bystanders were inspired by the UNI to help both George and the officers avoid a whole lot of suffering! It is safe to assume everyone involved in that situation was unaware/unable to hear the UCS warning bells and the situation was quickly escalating to become a Nasty-9 event. Therefore, the UNI took more drastic measures and inspired several bystanders to verbally and very clearly instruct the officers to get up, check George's pulse, and more.

Imagine how much suffering could have been avoided if everyone involved in that situation understood their UCS, intuitions, and inspirations?

Most people on the planet are unaware of how the UCS works. Consequently, they have focused incorrectly, ignored their intuitions and inspirations. This is why we have such chaos and suffering in the world.

* * *

"Hello! Are you in there? Would you like to come out and play with me?" said the pretty girl as she bent over and stuck her head in a burrow, in an attempt to speak with whatever creature was dwelling inside.

"This is exactly what your parents teach you not to do when you are hiking in the wilderness," I said, facetiously.

But that did not stop the girl. She was on a mission to enjoy nature to the fullest and nothing was going to stop her.

"She is from Australia after all and maybe she is related to Crocodile Dundee. How else do you explain what she is up to?" I thought as we continued our hike in Alaska.

Our Alaska cruise had docked at Skagway earlier in the morning. Just as my wife and I were about to leave the port to explore the city, we bumped into the girl. We had spoken with her on the cruise earlier and she seemed like a fun-loving free spirit. She decided to tag along with us, and as we started our hike together we realized how much of a free-spirit she really was. It was a perfect day for a hike in Alaska, misty with a slight drizzle that brought to life the breathtaking landscape even more.

It really was an amazing hike on its own, but our new companion made it so much more exciting. So far, we had seen her drink water from the leaves, scope out and eat vegetation off the ground, roll around the moss-covered ground in pure ecstasy, and stick her head into every burrow to speak with the creatures. We never knew what she was going to do next.

After an exciting and arduous hike on that brisk day, we finally reached the top and saw a pristine lake! We had reached our destination. The girl had an exceptionally unique reaction to the lake. She gasped and darted forwards. My wife and I looked at each other in amazement and a hint of disbelief. The girl jumped in the icy cold lake without a pause and swam around to her heart's content!

My wife and I sat by the lake and looked around to take it all in. An incredible hike, clean air, breathtaking landscape, and a frolicking friend in the lake. I thought ..

"Who needs a TV when life is this exciting!"

10

Media

> "*It is easier to hypnotize people than it is to convince them that they have been hypnotized.*"

Those words had the most profound impact on me ever since I first heard them during my training. **They are referring to the fact that most of us are already hypnotized by many sources we trust and even some that we do not trust. We live our lives under the spell of such hypnosis without even knowing it.**

After my training with The Amazing Kreskin, the UNI continued to introduce me to many more experts to learn from, including Joel Bauer and Marshall Sylver. My training in the fields of hypnosis, conditioning, suggestion, subliminal messaging, subconscious programming, persuasion, and body language continued through the last decade. It was clear that the UNI was preparing us for something.

What was the UNI preparing us for?

Just like a child who discovers a gun, thinks it is a toy and ends up shooting itself, humanity had discovered its most dangerous weapon and was about to shoot itself in the face with it. By the year 2010, the UNI already knew that humanity was heading for a once in a lifetime existential crisis and it was training us to be ready for it. You will understand these statements by the end of this chapter.

What I learned about the human mind was eye-opening, to say the least. For the first time in my life, I was aware of the monsters that had been manipulating my mind and I finally knew how to slay those monsters, free my mind, and reclaim my ability to think for myself. Media is one of those monsters.

Image courtesy of Google

My definition of media refers to any means of mass communication, including but not limited to newspapers, magazines, radio, television, music, internet, cell phones, computers, tablets, anything with internet connectivity, email, texting, messengers, social media, streaming services, people, and more.

Before my training, I thought that I could never be hypnotized. This is because I have a very logical mind and strong willpower. I always thought that only weak minds could be hypnotized. I was wrong. The research shows that intelligence, concentration, and focus determine how suggestible we are, not the strength of our minds. The fact is, we are all suggestible to a varying degree, depending on the topic. The topics where we are suggestible, we can easily be hypnotized. Here is my simplified definition of hypnosis: **Hypnosis occurs when we accept information as truth, without vetting it first.** Hypnosis, conditioning, suggestion, subliminal messaging, subconscious programming, persuasion, etc. are all branches of the same tree. The benefits of hypnosis are astounding when it is used for good. This is the reason hypnotherapy is used by the scientific community.

The process of hypnosis starts very early in our lives. When we are young and very suggestible, hypnosis comes from our parents. The tooth fairy is one such example of harmless hypnosis. As we get older, more sources are introduced including teachers, friends, religious leaders, political leaders, authority figures, newspapers, magazines, radio, television, music, internet, cell phones, computers, tablets, anything with internet connectivity, email, texting, messengers, social media, streaming services, and more. Unlike our parents, other sources may not have our best interests at heart and their hypnosis is not as harmless as the tooth fairy. When we accept information from such sources as truth without vetting it first, we start to form life-eroding beliefs. Our beliefs shape our personality, who we become, how we act, what we do, and how we live our lives. Our beliefs shape our reality because there are strong neural pathways associated with them. As you may recall, strong neural pathways have a strong pull associated with them. The fact is most of us have negative, life-eroding beliefs with negative pull associated with them. If our parents were poor and believed that rich people are evil, then it is likely they conditioned us to believe the same. That belief alone can keep us poor for the rest of our lives.

An apple does not fall far from the tree.

This is true because our parents teach us to believe as they have. Poor parents can not teach us to be rich. Hateful parents cannot teach us to be loving. Ignorant parents cannot teach us to be wise. If our beliefs and our thinking are the same as theirs, our results will be similar to theirs, unless we change our beliefs and thinking. This explains why we have such a large wealth gap in the world and concepts like "the top 1%" exist.

The media can easily condition you to believe things that are not true. They have the technology, resources, and wherewithal to do so. Let us look at some statistics regarding media usage.

In 2017 alone, an average U.S. consumer spent 238 minutes (3h 58min) daily watching TV.

According to a Nielsen report, United States adults are watching five hours and four minutes of television per day on average (35.5 h/week, slightly more than 77 days per year). Older people watch more (less than 50 h/week), younger people less (more than 20 h/week), both with a seasonal pattern that peaks in the winter months.

In 2009 the numbers were generally lower but still amounted to **9 years in front of the screen** for an average 65-year-old American (more than 4 h/day, 28 h/week). **An average child in the US will see 20,000 30-second TV commercials per year and will see over 2 million TV commercials by age 65.**

In a study of 1,452 high school students, **there was an association between what type of television was consumed and the effects each genre had** on the body image of an adolescent. It was found that time watching soap operas had a direct correlation with a drive to thinness in both genders, and also the drive for muscularity in boys. **Television usage has significant correlations to negative outcomes for both males and females.**

So much is written about the effects of media: https://bit.ly/33KqkGr

WOW!

Almost 10 years of our lives spent in front of screens wasting it away! More than the time wasted, the real issue is how we are being conditioned by the information, and how it governs the course of our lives. Remember, hypnosis is real enough that it is used scientifically in hypnotherapy. There are countless recorded cases of how effective hypnosis is. When we spend so much of our time focusing on a variety of topics where we are suggestible, the hypnosis is guaranteed to happen.

Remember my friends that argued viciously over their political beliefs?
Where do you think their beliefs came from?

Their beliefs came from the hypnosis of the media and the political leaders. Some of my friends believe the president is the Devil, and we are doomed if he gets re-elected. The others believe he is sent by God, and we are doomed if he does not get re-elected.

Aren't those contradicting beliefs a clear indication of political hypnosis?

My friends have done well in their lives. Yet they do not have the time or resources to fact-check the media that is manipulating their minds. My friends did not grow up with the president, they are not part of his family, they do not live with him, they do not work with him, they have never met him and most of them have never even physically seen him. These friends, just like most humans, are drawing all their conclusions based on the information presented by the media and from the political campaigns. They believe they can identify fake news by applying logic, critical thinking, and discernment.

Yeah, right!

The technology to produce media footage has advanced so much faster than our ability to fact-check. Even a teenager can create studio-quality and very persuasive content that even professionals would not be able to identify as fake.

Are you familiar with YouTube Space?

Being a tech professional, I have always admired how much technology has done to make our lives easier. One of my companies works with celebrities and I had a chance to examine YouTube's creative space near the Los Angeles International Airport. It was a massive hanger once owned by Howard Hughes. The YouTube spaces are locations around the world where creative people can produce great studio-quality content.

Almost a decade ago, that location in LA had several massive stages, 3 green screen studios, a motion capture studio, a rehearsal room/dance studio, a 47 person 4k resolution screening room, a 200 person outdoor amphitheater, an equipment bay for gear, and a post-production room for editing the videos. This facility was very impressive even that long ago.

Today YouTube Space has evolved into something so much more. In the past, making movies required millions of dollars and was a privilege, available only to a few. Thanks to YouTube, even a youngster can utilize technology used by movie studios and can create highly persuasive content. YouTube Space now has many locations around the world: https://bit.ly/34XY6aQ

I would also urge you to understand deep-fake technologies in your spare time: https://bit.ly/2FwpN1z

My friends cannot fact-check what they are accepting as truth. No one can fact-check all the content that is generated every day! Not billionaires, not governments, not anyone! **Even if we combined all**

human resources together, we would not be able to fact-check the content generated in even a single minute. It is impossible because of the amount of data we generate everyday!

According to the sixth edition of DOMO's report, and according to their research: https://bit.ly/2SWb2bv

"Over 2.5 quintillion bytes of data are created every single day, and it's only going to grow from there. By 2020, it's estimated that 1.7MB of data will be created every second for every person on earth."

It is estimated that 90% of the world's data has been created in the last two years: https://bit.ly/2T4geu2

Please review this infographic from DOMO's report:

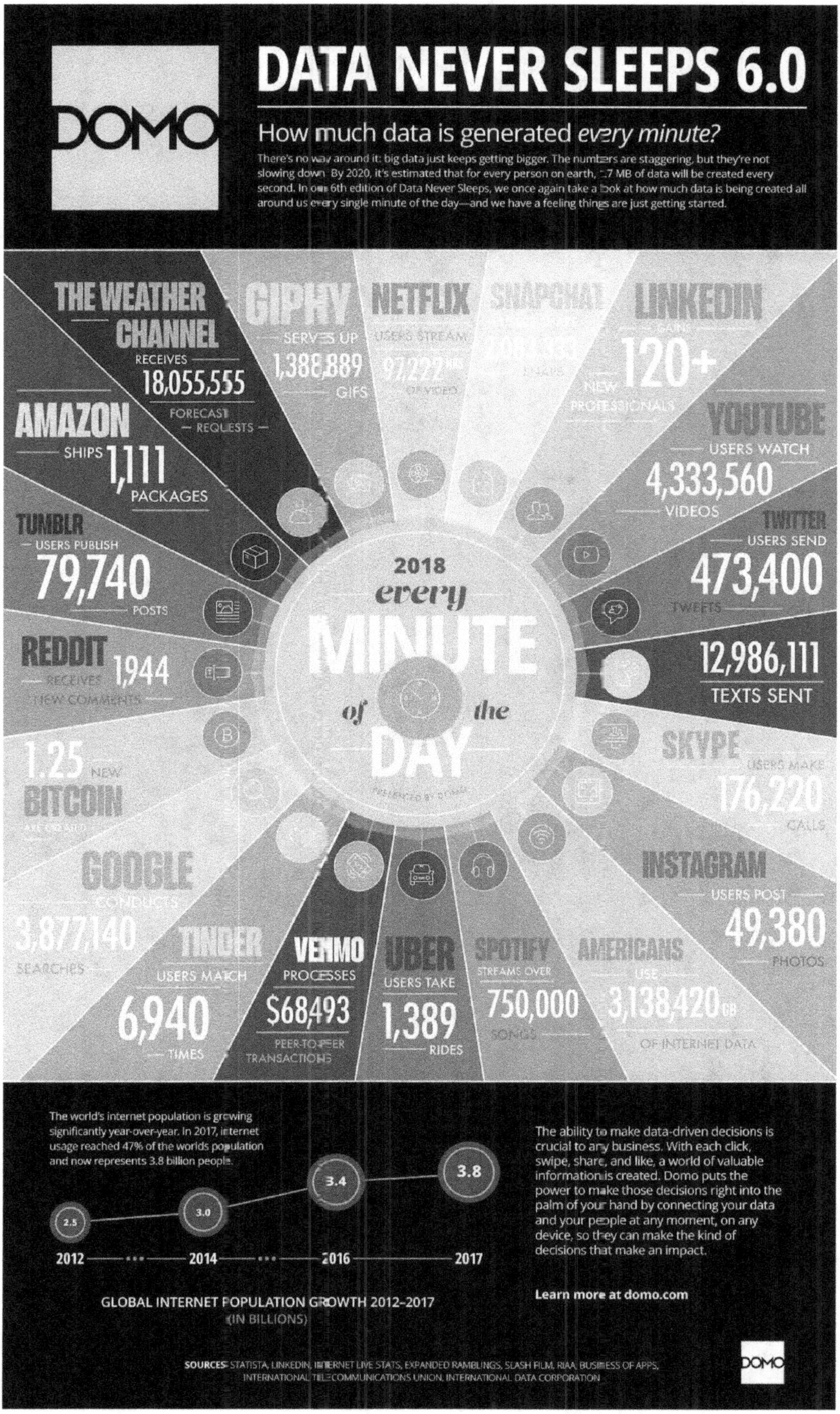
DOMO
DATA NEVER SLEEPS 6.0
How much data is generated every minute?
There's no way around it: big data just keeps getting bigger. The numbers are staggering, but they're not slowing down. By 2020, it's estimated that for every person on earth, 1.7 MB of data will be created every second. In our 6th edition of Data Never Sleeps, we once again take a look at how much data is being created all around us every single minute of the day—and we have a feeling things are just getting started.
THE WEATHER CHANNEL RECEIVES 18,055,555 FORECAST REQUESTS
GIPHY SERVES UP 1,388,889 GIFS
NETFLIX USERS STREAM 97,222 HRS OF VIDEO
SNAPCHAT
LINKEDIN GAINS 120+ NEW PROFESSIONALS
AMAZON SHIPS 1,111 PACKAGES
YOUTUBE USERS WATCH 4,333,560 VIDEOS
TUMBLR USERS PUBLISH 79,740 POSTS
TWITTER USERS SEND 473,400 TWEETS
2018 every MINUTE of the DAY
REDDIT RECEIVES 1944 NEW COMMENTS
12,986,111 TEXTS SENT
1.25 NEW BITCOIN ARE CREATED
SKYPE USERS MAKE 176,220 CALLS
GOOGLE CONDUCTS 3,877,140 SEARCHES
INSTAGRAM USERS POST 49,380 PHOTOS
TINDER USERS MATCH 6,940 TIMES
VENMO PROCESSES $68,493 PEER-TO-PEER TRANSACTIONS
UBER USERS TAKE 1,389 RIDES
SPOTIFY STREAMS OVER 750,000 SONGS
AMERICANS USE 3,138,420 GB OF INTERNET DATA
The world's internet population is growing significantly year-over-year. In 2017, internet usage reached 47% of the worlds population and now represents 3.8 billion people.
2.5
3.0
3.4
3.8
2012
2014
2016
2017
GLOBAL INTERNET POPULATION GROWTH 2012–2017 (IN BILLIONS)
The ability to make data-driven decisions is crucial to any business. With each click, swipe, share, and like, a world of valuable information is created. Domo puts the power to make those decisions right into the palm of your hand by connecting your data and your people at any moment, on any device, so they can make the kind of decisions that make an impact.
Learn more at domo.com
SOURCES: STATISTA, LINKEDIN, INTERNET LIVE STATS, EXPANDED RAMBLINGS, SLASH FILM, RIAA, BUSINESS OF APPS, INTERNATIONAL TELECOMMUNICATIONS UNION, INTERNATIONAL DATA CORPORATION
DOMO

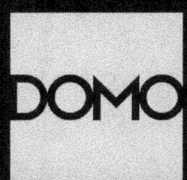

There is another big problem with consuming information from the media. This has to do with how our brain fills in the gaps because our physical senses are limited. Please take a look at this picture. Do you see the lighter color on the left and the darker color on the right?

Image courtesy of medicalxpress.com

Now take a solid, non-see-through object like a ruler and cover up the border in the middle which separates the two shades.

What kind of sorcery is this?
How did the color on both sides become the same?

The color was always the same. **It was the presentation that tricked your brain into filling the gaps:** https://bit.ly/2GyEAtm

Do you think the presentation of media in today's world may be tricking our brains into filling the gaps?

It is common knowledge that the media industry takes things out of context. We have all heard the term fake-news tossed around a lot in the past few years. The fact is, when we watch media presented in a certain fashion, our brains will fill in the gaps based on our belief system. Because we all have different beliefs, letting the brain fill in gaps will surely result in conflict, division, and chaos.

Need some proof?

When people saw the first video of George Floyd, recorded by the bystander, their brains filled in the gaps and made a lot of assumptions, based on their beliefs.

The result was conflict, division, hate, chaos, protests, riots, looting, suffering and so much more. It divided and crippled America!

Then the second video, recorded by the bodycam of one of the officers, was released much later after the damage was already done.

See for yourself what people had to say about it.

▮ 1 week ago
This is INSANE. Why wasn't this presented earlier? So much fake news has been spreaded already, it's too late now.

👍 1.5K 👎 REPLY

▮ 1 week ago
After seeing this video, I am never gonna believe what the media says ever again

👍 677 👎 REPLY

▾ View 28 replies

▮ 2 days ago
"If you don't watch the news you're uninformed.. if you do you're misinformed. The media doesn't care about being right.. just being first." - Denzel Washington

👍 90 👎 REPLY

▮ 2 days ago
This, my friends, is why I don't trust the media

👍 142 👎 REPLY

▮ 1 week ago
This proves media can really manipulate the minds of people, they can put up hate and racism for political propaganda!

👍 829 👎 REPLY

▮ 6 days ago
DEFUND THE MEDIA!!

👍 28 👎 REPLY

▮ 5 days ago
Did the media just create a race war and caused the rioting and looting

👍 66 👎 REPLY

▮ 2 days ago
The media is a disgrace.

👍 114 👎 REPLY

▮ 4 days ago
These are the kind of videos that the media are too afraid to expose after telling it wrong the first time

👍 255 👎 REPLY

▾ View 10 replies

▮ 1 week ago
I feel if this was released sooner half our country wouldn't be killing each other smfh

👍 1K 👎 REPLY

▾ View 98 replies

▮ 6 days ago
The media is the enemy of the people.

👍 295 👎 REPLY

▮ 1 week ago
The real question is "WHY WAS THIS NOT RELEASED EARLIER"? So many lives, properties have been destroyed over this? The real criminal is the person who did not sanction the video to be released earlier.

👍 2.2K 👎 REPLY

Image courtesy of Google

Now that you have some understanding of hypnosis, you are ready to understand what the UNI was protecting us from. Around the year 2010, the UNI was well aware that humanity had created its most dangerous manipulation engines that would be responsible for the unprecedented...

...mass rapes, mass killings, burning of entire villages, serious crimes against humanity, mass chaos, outrage, incivility, loneliness, depression, anxiety, suicides, alienation, polarization, remote-control warfare, violence, global assault on democracy, etc...

Those are words used to describe the mass manipulation engines that are responsible for the state of the world today. What is interesting is that most of those words are from the creators of these mass manipulation engines!

Image courtesy of The Social Dilemma Production

Allow me to introduce you to one of the greatest educational documentaries of our time, The Social Dilemma. This is a must-watch documentary for every person that uses a device with a screen in today's world. The next chapter will teach you how to eliminate the problem, but the solution depends on your understanding of the information presented in the documentary. At the time of writing this book, the documentary is available on Netflix. I am certain it will be available online at any given point. Find it and watch it now, even if you must pay for it!

11

Opinions and Approval

If you are reading this, I am going to assume you have finished watching the documentary. I am sure the following statements will make much more sense now:

- **As you get more beings to focus, the expansion becomes exponential.**
- **What happens in your world is a result of the collective focus of everyone regarding your world.**

The media's ability to get billions of beings to focus on horrible things is the reason why we have unprecedented chaos and suffering in the world. We have reached the destroyer-size negative pull on various global topics and the best solution is to correct our focus.

That is why this book is written!

Please understand that I am also a tech entrepreneur. I respect and love the power of technology and all the good that came out of the technology platforms. These platforms can also be used for incredibly positive changes in the world if you can get billions of people to focus correctly. In this chapter, I am going to emphasize several additional points to expand on what you have learned from the documentary, and then **you will be presented with a Law of Focus compliant solutions to use the power of media for good.**

Based on what you learned from the documentary, have you noticed something different about the leaders of today?

Let us take a look at a couple of leaders from the past:

Washington the Soldier Lieutenant Colonel Washington on horseback during the Battle of the Monongahela (oil, Regnier, 1834).
Image courtesy of Wikipedia

The next picture is Gandhi leading his followers on the famous salt march to break the English Salt Laws.

Image courtesy of Wikipedia

These leaders of the past were actually in the vanguard, leading people, and **risking their lives for what they believed in!** And both Gandhi and George Washington did not hold on to power once they accomplished what they set out to do. These leaders of the past assumed all the risks, lived by example, and set the standard for how a leader should be.

Political leaders of today do not have any skin in the game. They enjoy the benefits of being in a power position but do not risk much in return. They hide behind security detail, fortified vehicles, buildings, and bunkers; all paid for by the people. From these secure places, they use the power of the media to manipulate and hypnotize the masses with their propaganda (hypnosis). They will compel the masses to take action and right the wrongs, but you will never see them marching alongside the people to right the wrongs. Some of the victims of their hypnosis, will turn on their friends, family, neighbors, and commit acts of atrocities, all based on the misinformation they accepted as truth without vetting it! Many such victims are sitting in jail today, wondering how they got there. Sadly, they will never realize that they were hypnotized by someone very persuasive. If you study the subconscious mind enough, you will realize that the leaders of today are masters of persuasion and nothing more and the victims of their hypnosis have paid a hefty price.

So, what would be the outcome of the destroyer-size negative pull associated with US politics?

Well, there is no chance the elections will be smooth. Regardless of who wins, there will be chaos, violence, destruction, and suffering. Everyone that has focused incorrectly will be impacted negatively to the degree of their incorrect focus. People at the height of their incorrect focus will become the puppets of the pull and will be compelled to engage in harmful activities. Many will end up in jail. **The saddest part is that the victims of this suffering will never realize that they were hypnotized by someone to focus incorrectly and they could have avoided the suffering simply by correcting their focus early on.** Also, the misinformation pandemic will certainly lead to further division of the country.

Now let us address two additional relevant topics; opinions and approval.

Have you heard the story of the elephant and the blind men?

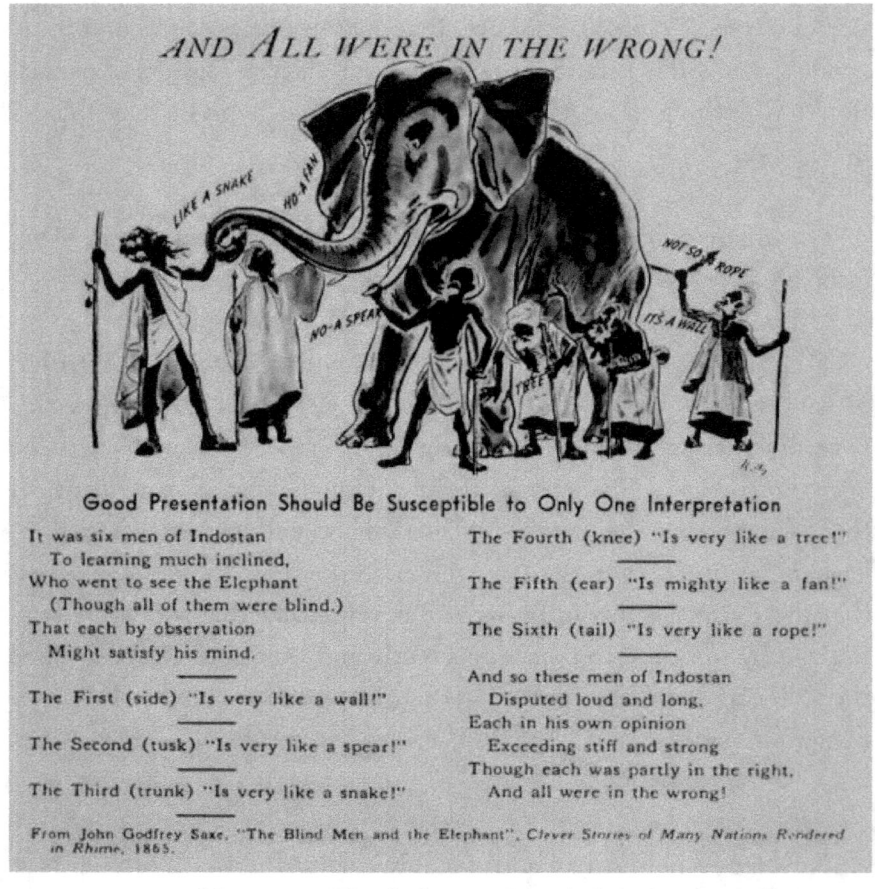

A poem version of the concept, "The Blind Men and the Elephant" by John Godfrey Saxe (1816–1887). The graphic from the book by Willard C. Brinton.
Image courtesy of Wikipedia.

The tale of the Blind Men and an Elephant originated in India and then spread throughout the ancient cultures because of the valuable message it carried. It is a story of blind men who come across an elephant and conceptualize the elephant with only the senses available to them. They are blind and cannot see the whole elephant, so they touch only a part of it and assume it represents the whole elephant. They then describe the elephant based on their limited experience and their descriptions of the elephant are different from each other. They suspect that the others are dishonest, and they do what humans are known for, fight over who is right! **The moral of the story is we tend to claim ab-**

solute truth based on our limited, subjective experience as we ignore other people's limited, subjective experiences which are equally true.

That last sentence sums up why we have conflict in the world! Whether it is a political, religious, military, or any other kind of conflict, it spawns from the fact that fully grown intellectual humans, with their diplomas, degrees, and PhDs, do not understand such a simple concept which was documented in a book (Rigveda) over 3,500 (~1,500 BCE) years ago.

Why was it put into Rigveda that long ago?

Because the wise men back then were baffled by the buffoons bickering over opinions!

After watching the documentary, I am sure you have realized that all conflict is a result of the differences in opinions and social media has been misused for the nefarious purpose of exploiting the differences in opinions to destabilize the world.

Understanding how opinions are formed and what to do with them is a requirement to work with the UNI. It is important to understand that our senses do not interpret reality as it truly is. You may remember the example of the vase proving how your brain fills in the gaps when you observe things with your eyes. The brain does that with all the physical senses: sight, sound, smell, taste, and touch.

Are you familiar with the electromagnetic spectrum?

The electromagnetic spectrum is the range of frequencies (the spectrum) of electromagnetic radiation and their respective wavelengths and photon energies: https://bit.ly/3jQhKvu

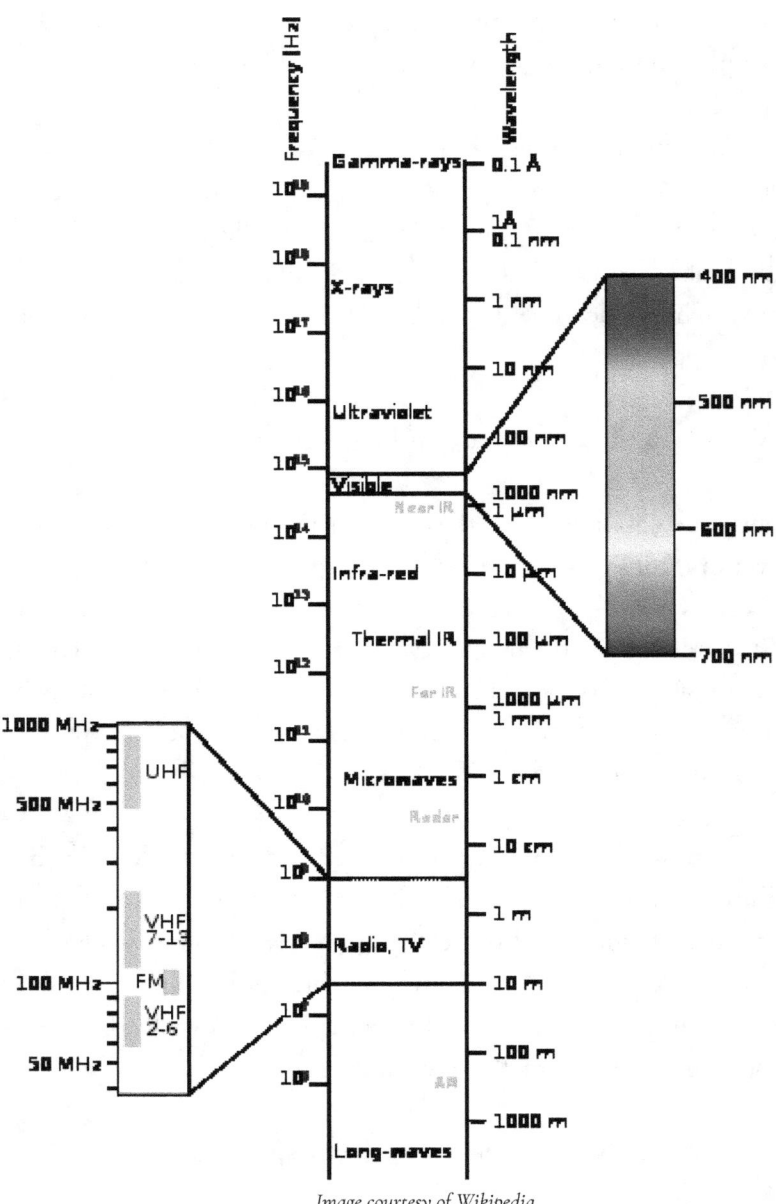

Image courtesy of Wikipedia

Do you see the tiny section labeled "Visible" from 400nm-700nm?

That is the small section of the entire range visible to our eyes. There are so many more frequencies out there that we cannot see with our eyes.

Are you familiar with dog whistles?

A dog whistle (also known as a silent whistle or Galton's whistle) is a type of whistle **that emits sound in the ultrasonic range, which most humans cannot hear but some other animals can,** including dogs and domestic cats, and is used in their training. This is an example of how our ears cannot hear certain sounds. The sonogram is another example of sounds that humans cannot hear.

We also know that our noses cannot smell everything that a hound can. The point I am making is of great importance:

Because our senses are limited, our perception of reality is faulty.
Based on that faulty reality, we form faulty opinions.
We shamelessly share these faulty opinions with others like it's candy.
Sometimes we impose these faulty opinions on others.
With enough repetitions, these faulty opinions turn into faulty beliefs.
We waste so much time & energy imposing our faulty beliefs on others.
When others disagree, because their faulty opinions & beliefs are different than our own faulty opinions & beliefs; we argue, fight, start wars, or do whatever it takes to prove that our faulty opinions & beliefs are...hmmm...should I say...better than their faulty opinions & beliefs!

Just look around the internet and you will find opinions wreaking havoc everywhere. It seems the world has engaged in opinion wars. You will find both rave reviews and horrible reviews for virtually everything. I saw two bad reviews for the same restaurant, one because they required masks and another because they did not promote masks enough! I am certain that if God wrote a book today to help mankind, it will offend some people and will surely have some bad reviews. Please consider the fact that one can never condemn, criticize or leave a bad review without one's UCS firing a warning bell. It is so because one's focus on condemnation, criticism, or writing a bad review will alert the Law of Focus to queue up more bad experiences. That is the reason prophets and religions emphasize concepts such as "judge not". **You get more of what you focus on.**

So, what is the correct way to deal with opinions?

Accept the fact that our opinions are not meant to be imposed on others. If you stop imposing your opinions on others, virtually all of your suffering will be eliminated! Also, you must not let the opinions of others bother you because they are faulty too. When the opinions of others stop bothering you, you will achieve lasting peace! Our opinions only prove how we have interpreted our reality, and the opinions of others only prove how they have interpreted the same reality. I am not saying you can never state your opinions. Just understand that you are stating opinions and not the truth and do not waste your energy arguing over opinions.

Is it possible to form accurate opinions?
Is it possible to interpret our reality more accurately?

We cannot interpret our reality accurately using just five of our senses. We must include our sixth sense, the UCS, to see a more complete picture. The problem is, most of us were never taught to utilize the UCS in opinion-forming. Therefore, we may have been doing it incorrectly our entire lives, leading to faulty opinions. As you have learned already, the UNI knows the true reality, and utilizing your UCS will allow you to form more accurate opinions.

How do you utilize the UCS for opinion-forming?

Just be aware of what the UCS is indicating while forming your opinions. Recently, one of my friends stated that we are doomed if the politician of her choice is not elected president. Her body language showed clear signs of fear, indicating a UCS warning while she was stating her opinion. That means her UCS does not agree and she will not be doomed even if the politician of her choice is not elected president. Correct your opinions (thoughts) until you feel a Fan-14 and you will have formed a valid opinion. **Correct your opinions (thoughts) until you feel a Fab-5 and you will have formed the most accurate opinion.** Here is an opinion that evokes a Fan-14 from me:

"I have learned through my experiences that the UNI is the most powerful, most loving, most sophisticated entity ever. The UNI can protect me better than anyone and I feel safe under that protection. Everything gets better and better for me regardless of what is going on in the world. It does not matter who the leader of the country is as long as I am led by the UNI."

Now, let us discuss the issue of approval.

Because we know deep down that our opinions are faulty, we subconsciously try to validate them by getting other people's approval. The rationale here is that if others also agree, then our opinions cannot be invalid. This need for approval is one of the reasons behind the rise of mass manipulation engines. If we get enough likes, then we have the much-needed approval. This is a behavior that must be eliminated if you wish to work with the UNI. That means you may have to identify and eliminate all habits that require approval and not just social media habits.

Approval of our UCS is the only approval we need!

Now, it is time to free your most important asset, your mind, from the control of the media!

Are you ready?

While there is nothing on this planet that can fact-check everything, you are already equipped with something that does fact-check everything! The UNI already knows the what, when, where, who, how, and why of all media content. **The UNI systems can process all media content instantaneously and separate the facts from fiction.**

Need some proof?

Try this experiment, but only once. Pick a politician you love and watch a video that severely bashes him. Observe how many UCS warning bells are fired when your beliefs clash with your UCS. Most of us have many beliefs we have made up about our politicians. When our beliefs conflict with the information presented in the video, we automatically reject it with negative thoughts. If the UCS does not agree with those thoughts, it will fire a warning bell.

Are you suggesting that I can consume media as long as I utilize my UCS?

No! There is a destroyer size negative pull associated with most media content. Watching content with the destroyer size negative pull will simply grab you by the gullet and have its way with you! Generally speaking, even glancing at news headlines triggers a UCS warning bell. The majority of the emotions we feel while consuming the media are not Fan-14, which indicates a UCS warning bell. Remember, just holding the word "HATE" in your hand makes you weak. Imagine the impact of holding so much hateful content in your mind. It is what holds you back from creating the life of your dreams.

Remember how I had asked you to eliminate anything with the destroyer size negative pull from your life?

I am now asking you to eliminate the media from your life altogether! Remember, some sacrifices must be made to work with the UNI. **A lifetime worth of false beliefs cannot be washed away unless you take some time away from the media.** I know it seems impossible for some of you.

How would I be informed?
Isn't it dangerous to cutoff media?
What if I rely on the media to make a living?
Are you asking me to stick my head in the sand and pretend everything is fine?

The truth is you do not need the media to live your life. I have been disconnected for over a decade. I gave up media altogether and used that time to create the life of my choosing. Within a decade, I went from an unhappy employee to starting my companies, manifesting enough money, and retiring. That is what happens when you focus correctly. During that time, I did not use media for anything other than business and never even signed up for social media. I am virtually a ghost on the internet with only the footprint needed for my businesses. I understand that you may have to use some media for work and other purposes to sustain life, and that is allowed. Even today, I do not have a TV, yet I am informed as needed by the UNI agents.

If a hurricane is heading our way, UNI sends agents to notify us.
If a problem needs solving, we receive the solution via our intuition.
If an action is required, we are inspired to take that action.

If we continue the media usage, we can never reach a point where we can identify UNI agents, recognize our intuitions, and follow-through on our inspirations. These subtle signals are overshadowed by excessive media stimulus. We have approximately 60,000 to 80,000 thoughts per day. Most of them are resulting from the media stimulus. **There is no way we can separate intuitions and inspiration from that pile of garbage unless we eliminate the media.**

Imagine what would happen if all your thoughts were about the life of your choosing?

If you focused on the life of your choosing with over 60,000 thoughts a day, the Law of Focus would turn the life of your choosing into a reality so fast, it would knock your socks off!

I understand it is not easy to give up media. We live in a world where so many children are raised by the media. The cold turkey approach can work with some people. But, if you struggle with the cold turkey approach, then do it gradually. Try it for a minimum of 100 days. You will be amazed by the results.

Believe me when I say you do not need the media to be entertained. The UNI can keep you entertained in ways you cannot even imagine. Once you have survived the media detox for at least 100 days, you can utilize the power of the media for good. Media is a powerful tool and can be used to create a life of your choosing. Thanks to the rise of streaming platforms and media warehouses, we now have access to content on demand. After your detox, you can use the on-demand content, **in a limited, controlled** fashion as long as you follow this one rule.

The media content must evoke a Fab-5 from you!

Here are some examples of content that evokes Fab-5 from us:

- Content that gives us a good belly laugh.
- Content that expands our minds. We love the "Top 10..." lists on YouTube such as "Top 10 Amazing Homes", "Top 10 Amazing

Cars", "Top 10 Amazing Hotels", "Top 10 Best Restaurants", "Top 10 Best Islands", etc.
- Content that shows human potential in a good light. "Top 10 Unforgettable Golden Buzzers on America's Got Talent", "People Are Awesome", "Amazing People Doing Amazing Things", etc.
- Content that is in harmony with our desires. We love to travel. Because global travel is shut down, we are virtually visiting two countries every day until we have finished visiting the 196 countries on our list. Every evening, my wife and I select one country each. Then, we find a high-resolution video of the top 10 best places to visit in that country. After, we rate the countries to determine which ones we want to visit once travel resumes again. This process will take us almost four months to complete, and once it is finished, we will come up with a different game to play.

Be creative in your media usage but also **be honest about what your UCS is telling you.** When you focus on good digital content that evokes a Fab-5 from you, you are using the power of the media correctly and you will get to the life of your choosing much faster. For the first time in my life, I am on social media now, only to connect with the readers of this book. You can find me on Instagram (@pandemic_to_peace or https://bit.ly/3m3QPgC) or email me at pandemictopeace@gmail.com.

* * *

"My family has a place on the beach in Hilton Head Island. You should stop by on your way down. We will already be there, and we can meet up again," said our friend as we stuffed our faces. We chuckled as we recognized him as a UNI agent, inspired to utter those words. This was on day eight of our three-week road trip as we were visiting our friend's beautiful house on the bay in New Rochelle. You may remember that New Rochelle, New York was the ground zero for coronavirus in America. We were not worried because we are under the protection of the UNI during this road trip. So far, we were having a fantastic evening

with our friends. We ate delicious ripe berries right off the tree, lit a fire, barbequed, and experimented with Mystical Fire.

We left the town of Natural Bridge and made our way to Hilton Head Island because we had accepted my friend's invitation to reunite on our way down. When we arrived around noon, we were quite hungry, so we decided to grab lunch before going to the condo. My wife is a vegan and I am mostly vegan, so we found a vegan restaurant called "Delishee Yo". It was incredible to see that most of their produce came from the organically farmed garden right outside their window. See below an excerpt from their website: https://bit.ly/3j2DOlt

> "We have a whopping 0.07-acre lot where we grow, harvest, prep, and serve our fruits and vegetables. Our produce is organic and always within sight of our kitchen window. There are about 34 steps between the kale growing in the garden and the salad bar, where we prepare our massaged kale salad. Food that fresh has about double the nutritional value of imported foods."

Image courtesy of delisheeyo.com

While enjoying their delicious and nutritious kale chips, I thought...

"Who says you have to sacrifice taste to eat **healthily**?"

12

Health

Without a healthy mind, there cannot be a healthy body and without a healthy body, it is hard to have a healthy mind. It is a paradox. The bottom line is that a healthy body and mind are necessary to produce the best results when working with the UNI. **An unhealthy body will cause distortion and interfere with your UCS signals, intuitions, and inspirations.**

So much has been written about health by so many experts. For the past several decades, we have taken a deep interest in our health and wellness. Through a lot of research and experiments, we have come to conclusions on what worked and what did not for us. I will summarize these conclusions now to make your wellness journey easier. But, before we go any further, let us review this disclaimer:

None of the statements in this book have been evaluated by the Food and Drug Administration. Nothing mentioned in this book is intended to diagnose, treat, cure, or prevent any diseases. Furthermore, none of the statements in this book should be construed as dispensing medical advice, making claims regarding the cure of diseases. You should consult a licensed health care professional before starting any supplement, dietary, or exercise program, especially if you are pregnant or have any pre-existing injuries or medical conditions. I simply present my opinions and nothing more.

Health, peace, prosperity, happiness, and success all begin within. What most people fail to realize (and conventional allopathic medicine failed to realize for a significant portion of its existence), is that the food, water, and nutrition that you put in your body affects everything from how you feel to what you think to how long you live. Over the last 25 years, significant medical research has been conducted on the effects of various foods, nutrients, and water on our health. And the discoveries have been amazing. With everything we put in our mouths, we are either amplifying our focus, joy, and lifespan or reducing it. In other words, we are either enhancing our lives or eroding them. As you have learned, your focus creates your reality. Therefore, your lifestyle must work to enhance and strengthen your focus. **This begins with what you eat and drink, is amplified by the supplements you take, and is perfected with little habits that make a big difference.** Any discussion on health must begin with the things that are wreaking havoc on our health. Simply by eliminating or reducing these things, we will notice a drastic difference in our lives. We will follow this up by including tips on what to eat to help our bodies and minds thrive and take our health to the next level with proper supplementation. Lastly, we will cover some small habits that can make a big change in our lives.

WHAT TO ELIMINATE

Tap water:
The water is meant to be healing and it is very healing if it has a high number of Totally Dissolved Solids (TDS) that are good for the body. The problem is, most of the drinking water contains a high number

of bad TDS. This is an unfortunate side effect of human evolution. As we evolved, we created harmful chemicals, and carelessly released them into the environment. As a result, our water, air, and food are polluted. In 2014, officials from Flint, Michigan switched the city's water supply to the Flint River as a cost-cutting measure for the struggling city. In doing so, they unwittingly introduced lead-poisoned water into homes, in what would become a massive public-health crisis. In August 2020, Michigan was fined to pay $600 million in the Flint water crisis settlement. The crisis in Flint, Michigan is a perfect example of how careless we are with our essential needs.

The water that comes from your tap contains hundreds of toxic chemicals from lead to arsenic to chlorine to fluoride. Each of these has various deleterious effects on your brain function and your health. Water is chlorinated to kill bacteria and pathogens, but when we drink that chlorinated water it wipes out the crucially beneficial bacteria in our intestines which play a vital role in our health and well-being. Fluoride is also a potent neurotoxin, and studies have shown associations between fluoride and lower IQs in children. Heavy metals like lead, mercury, and arsenic truly do not have any "safe" levels and disrupt health even at the allowed amounts in our tap water.

How to eliminate:
Use a reverse osmosis filtration system in your house or buy filters that will remove fluoride in addition to the other chemicals (keep in mind most conventional carbon filters do not remove fluoride). Alternatives include spring water, aquifer water, and glacier water. If you live near a pristine spring, aquifer, or glacier, and can utilize that water, then you are good to go. I am not suggesting buying bottled water labeled as spring, aquifer, or glacier water unless you have a way to verify those claims. This is how I prepare my water:

- My "iSpring 6-Stage RO" system uses the first 5-stages to remove the bad TDS and then adds some of the good TDS back to the water: http://bit.ly/ispring6water The conflict around RO water is that it takes out even the good TDS to clean the water. This is no longer true. Some of the good TDS are added back into the water by this system and the rest of the mineral needs for my body are fulfilled by the diet and supplements mentioned in this chapter.

- I store the RO water in a clean copper vessel with a set of nine Chakra crystals to imprint the water with proper vibration/energy. These crystals are Amethyst, Rose Quartz, Lapis Lazuli, Clear Quartz, Aventurine, Obsidian, Red Jasper, Tiger's Eye, and Yellow Jade. Water sits in the vessel until we use it for drinking and cooking. This step is valuable as proven by recent research. Internationally renowned Japanese scientist Masaru Emoto's research visually captured the structure of water at the moment of freezing, and through high-speed photography, he showed the direct consequences of destructive thoughts and the thoughts of love and appreciation on the formation of water crystals. The energy of the Chakra crystals will change the water vibration for the better. For more information, read Masaru Emoto's book: https://amzn.to/34Y7b38

There is value in investing in a good shower filter as well.

Monosodium Glutamate (MSG):

This highly toxic chemical is used widely throughout mainstream products from chips to soups to restaurant food. What monosodium glutamate does is trick your taste buds into thinking what you are eating is tasty. This allows manufacturers to produce cheap, low-quality products that are addictive to your taste buds. It can disrupt your endocrine system, cause headaches, and damage neurons through its excitotoxicity (meaning it overstimulates the neurons to the point that they damage themselves).

How to eliminate:

Google "different names for MSG" to first learn all the names for MSG. Read food labels to eliminate anything with MSG. Buying only organic also eliminates the risk of MSG-laden products.

High Fructose Corn Syrup (HFCS):

This ubiquitous sweetener is derived from genetically modified corn and is considered one of the major contributing factors to the obesity epidemic today. Because the sweetener is, as the name implies, high in fructose, your brain never gets the signal from your body that it is full, leading you to eat more and more. Also, fructose is a highly inflammatory form of sugar, and inflammation is linked to most chronic illnesses that exist today.

How to eliminate:

Google "different names for high fructose corn syrup" to first learn all the names for HFCS. Read food labels to eliminate anything with HFCS. Buying only organic also eliminates the risk of HFCS-laden products.

Pesticides:

If I sprayed your apple with roach killer and asked you to wash it and eat it, would you?

Yet most people make that decision every single day by eating conventionally grown produce that is sprayed with pesticides 10-100 times stronger than the bug killers you buy at the store. Pesticides have been exposed to a wealth of studies to be carcinogenic, neurotoxic, and more. They contribute to weight gain, obesity, depression, anxiety, chronic disease, and poor overall health. They also disturb the balance of your gut and kill your healthy gut bacteria.

How to eliminate:

Only buy organic produce.

Chemicals:

As mankind advanced, we have introduced more and more harmful chemicals to our environment. From our vehicles to houses to food, water, and air, we are surrounded by chemicals. Many of these chemicals have so many harmful side-effects, have been linked to causing diseases, and wreak havoc on our health. Some of the worst chemicals we encounter are in our cleaning supplies. Avoid these!! They are poison. A recent study showed that people with high exposure to chemical cleansers had equivalent lung damage to smoking a pack of cigarettes a day for 20 years. Think about that.

How to eliminate:

Use natural materials, products, and alternatives in your environment. Products made of glass, wood, ceramic, steel, silver, gold, copper, or clay without lining are best for food/water storage. With some research, you can find tons of natural alternatives for everything. Educate yourself in your free time.

https://bit.ly/3jKaG3q
https://bit.ly/3461in

Artificial Sweeteners:

Aspartame is a highly toxic chemical sweetener that has been linked to a laundry list of detrimental effects. Studies have shown evidence of neurotoxicity, detrimental effects on mood, and cancer-promoting properties. Sucralose is almost equally as toxic, breaking down into highly toxic dioxins that have lasting damage to our health. The toxicity of these compounds is the reason they have both been linked to weight gain rather than weight loss despite being zero calories sweeteners.

How to eliminate:

Read your food and drink labels and replace your sweeteners with monk fruit or stevia leaf. We use "Organic Better Stevia Liquid" sweetener: http://bit.ly/stevia123

Gluten:

Gluten is the sticky protein found in wheat and rye. It has garnered significant attention over the last decade and has been popularized in the mainstream by well-known books such as The Grain Brain and Wheat Belly. Gluten is a highly inflammatory protein that irritates and inflames your gut, causing poor nutrient absorption, nerve damage, and more. Moreover, the wheat we eat today is far from the ancient wheat humans ate just 100 years ago. Our wheat has been hybridized to contain over 100 times the gluten content as natural wheat because gluten is addictive. There is a wealth of evidence about the damaging effects of gluten on both our digestion and our brains. Gluten is a neurotoxin that produces opioid-like effects in our brains both numbing out our nerves and creating an addictive attachment to our gluten-containing grains. It also leads to poor focus, irritability, mood disorders, and more. This severely impairs our ability to create the life of our choosing.

How to eliminate:

Find gluten-free grain products and use healthier gluten-free options in your cooking such as millet, sorghum, amaranth, buckwheat, quinoa, rice, coconut, flax, and more.

Dairy:

We tend to gloss over the fact that cow's milk was never intended for humans to consume. Milk and other dairy products have several major problems. First, most of the world's population loses the ability to process lactose, the sugar in milk, right after weaning. That unprocessed lactose causes inflammation and bloating in your GI tract and disturbs your healthy gut bacteria leading to a host of health problems. This is nature's way of telling us we were not meant to drink milk beyond the breast milk we have as an infant. There are also no other species of animals that drink milk after weaning.

Why is that?

Milk contains high levels of growth hormone and IGF-1, which are meant to make a baby grow rapidly so it is not eaten or attacked by predators. But continuing to drink milk and get exposed to high levels of IGF-1 promotes cancer, obesity, and premature aging/death. The third reason we should not consume dairy products is that they contain cow microRNAs, pieces of genetic material that are incompatible with our bodies that disrupt our hormonal balances and promote obesity, and early puberty. Lastly, the casein A1 protein found in most milk is immunogenic and has been theorized to be a contributing factor to type 1 diabetes. The list can continue, but you get the idea.

How to eliminate:

Replace dairy products, cheese, yogurt products, and even ice cream and replace them with plant-based products. Our favorite milk is "Califia Farms - Oat Milk, Unsweetened Barista Blend": http://bit.ly/oatcalifa

Meat:

If you look at the longest-lived cultures on the planet (located in the "blue zones"), not even one eats meat regularly. Studies have shown again and again that vegetarians live longer than meat-eaters and have reduced chronic disease and health risks such as colon cancer, high blood pressure, heart disease, and high cholesterol. The atrocities of factory farming aside, there are not many reasons that humans today need meat in their diets. The conventional reasoning behind meat consumption is that it is a good source of protein. Yet, studies show higher protein intake is correlated with higher rates of cancer and inflammation and that is one of the reasons vegetarians live longer and healthier lives on average than meat-eaters. When people learn that we are vegan they always ask how we get our protein. I tell them that I get my protein the same way as the biggest and strongest animals on the planet, from a plant-based diet. Please watch a myth-buster documentary called "The Game Changers" which shows that some of the best athletes on the planet achieved their record-breaking feats because they were on a plant-based diet. The documentary is rated TV-MA and is for Mature Audiences only due to some language and scenes. The documentary also points out media hypnosis relevant to the topic of food.

If one does choose to continue eating meat, the best practices are to limit consumption to one or two times a week and select grass-fed, free-range, organic meat sources.

ADD TO YOUR DIET

Fruits and Vegetables:
Fruits and vegetables are the most nutritionally beneficial foods that exist. They nourish your body with crucial vitamins and minerals, provide powerful antioxidants and anti-aging compounds, and are a rich source of gut nourishing fiber. Since we have to put the water through Reverse Osmosis to eliminate bad TDS, we also end up eliminating the good TDS. Therefore, fruits and vegetables are more essential now than ever before. The more fruits and vegetables you can get in your diet, the better. Choose organic whenever possible to avoid highly toxic pesticides, waxing, irradiation, and more.

Spices:
Spices are wonderful additions to food, both for our taste buds and our health. Almost all spices contain beneficial medicinal properties and can help your body and mind thrive. Again, choose organic spices whenever possible and you will taste the difference in freshness and potency.

Nuts:
Nuts are a powerful source of high-quality nutrition. Walnuts and almonds are brain superfoods that enhance your cognition and ability

to focus as well as keep your brain healthy for the long run. Brazil nuts, pistachios, macadamia nuts, etc. are all great as well. Avoid peanuts and cashews, both of which are not nuts and high in gut damaging lectins.

Healthy Oils:

It is a myth that fat is bad for you. Fat is vital for our brain and our cells and a look at the longest-lived cultures on earth (located in the "blue zones") reveals that the majority have high fat, low protein diets (the opposite of the typical American diet). The problem with fats is getting them from the right sources. Plant-based sources of healthy fats are much more beneficial than animal-based sources of fats. And when it concerns oils, far and away the healthiest oil is olive oil. Make sure it is organic, cold-pressed, and extra virgin. Other great oils include coconut oil, avocado oil, sesame oil, and almond oil. Avoid vegetable oils like the plague including soybean, corn, and peanut oils. Vegetable oils are almost always genetically modified and high in inflammatory omega-6 fatty acids.

Healthy Grains:

Healthy grains essentially mean all of the non-gluten containing grains. The most common gluten-containing grains to avoid are wheat and rye. Instead, you can incorporate other richly nutritious grains like sorghum, millet, quinoa, rice, amaranth, and buckwheat.

Lentils and Beans:

Lentils and beans are richly nutritious sources of protein, fiber, and minerals. Use them in abundance but remember to pressure cook them whenever possible. Pressure cooking eliminates lectins (which are anti-nutrients that are damaging to your digestive tract).

Supplements:

One of the blessings of our modern era is our ability to leverage the power of supplements. This has been done throughout history in various ways using special teas, nutritional herbs, and more. There are multiple ways to understand the power of supplements. First, they can assure you that you are getting complete nutrition daily that virtually no diet can support. Second, the right supplements can take your health and your success quotient to the next level. **When our brains have access to optimal nutrition and cognition supporting compounds, we access levels of focus and stamina consistently that we did not even know were possible before.** Similarly, it is theorized that humans began to evolve higher intelligence to form civilizations and more complex societies when they got access to brain supporting foods containing Docosahexaenoic acid, more popularly known as DHA. DHA makes up a significant portion of human brains and can support brain health and function. As we increased the level of DHA in our diets, we increased our ability for higher-level thinking because the machine (our brain) had finally gotten the fuel it needed (the DHA). The right supplements offer that same opportunity for taking you to a higher level. As someone who has tested tons of supplements over many years, I have firsthand experience with what works and what does not.

So, what are the right supplements?

First, let us go over some things you need to know about supplements in general.

Avoid supplements with any of the following ingredients:

- Magnesium stearate, stearic acid, gelatin, propylene glycol, aspartame, sucralose, GMOs, vanillin, EDTA, and FD&C food colors. All of these are toxic compounds that counteract any of the benefits these supplements may have or compounds that can inhibit the absorption of your supplements.
- Look for companies that tell you exactly how much of each ingredient is contained on the ingredients label. Many companies hide behind proprietary blends in which the amount of the actual ingredients is never revealed, and you never know if the

blend contains 99% of the cheap unimportant ingredients and only 1% of the good ones.
- Look for supplements with trademarked ingredients. These are the highest quality ingredients with proven research, purity, and potency. These ingredients will typically be followed with a ® or a ™.
- Look for companies that have lab testing of their supplements. This assures you that your supplements are giving you what they claim. Usually, you can find this on the labels or the company's website as a certification saying lab tested. Other beneficial certifications are produced in the USA, FDA registered facilities, and GMP certification.

Now that you know the basics let us briefly cover some of the supplements I would highly recommend.

Vitamin D3:

Over 40% of Americans are deficient in this vitamin that we get both from the sun and our diets. Vitamin D plays a very important role in our immune health, brain health, and moods. Given our indoor lifestyles, it is nearly impossible outside of the summer months to get enough vitamin D naturally, therefore, we could all benefit from daily vitamin D supplements. Aim for between 2000-3000 IU a day.

B-complex:

Necessary for our body to generate energy and help us cope with stress. Get a supplement with at least 100% of the daily value of vitamin B1, B2, B3, B5, B7, B9, and B12. A higher dose of B12 between 5000-15000% can be very beneficial and support both brain function and mood.

Alpha-GPC:

Alpha-GPC is a powerful natural cognition booster that helps enhance your focus and memory while also increasing your energy. Alpha-

GPC is a highly bioavailable form of choline, the crucial brain nutrient found in eggs. Choline helps make the neurotransmitter acetylcholine which is necessary for memory formation and mood regulation as well as many other functions in your brain and body. Look for at least 250 mg in a supplement. Other powerful brain health supplements include phosphatidylserine, bacopa monnieri, and pterostilbene.

Resveratrol:

This powerful anti-aging supplement became famous when it was discovered that it could potentially lengthen lifespan. Found in red wine, the skin of grapes, and blueberries, resveratrol is from a class of compounds called polyphenols. But resveratrol contains special properties that can slow the process of aging and potentially lengthen a healthy lifespan by three to ten years! In addition, it has benefits for your focus, your mood, and your heart health. The only problem with resveratrol is the amount contained directly in foods is minuscule and even in supplement form, only 20% is absorbed. Find a resveratrol supplement combined with piperine extract from black pepper which has shown to significantly increase blood levels and absorption. Ideally, find a supplement that provides at least 250-300 mg.

Astaxanthin:

Astaxanthin is the pigment that gives flamingoes and certain fish their color. This bright reddish-orange pigment is one of the strongest antioxidants known to man. It is over 6000 times more powerful than vitamin C and has significant benefits for your skin and eye health as well as your brain health because it can cross the blood-brain barrier and protect your nerves from oxidative damage. Look for a supplement with at least 3 mg.

Probiotics:

Our health begins and ends in our gut. Over 100 trillion bacteria live in our gut, which is ten times more than the number of human cells in our body. Eating probiotic-rich foods and taking a probiotic supplement is one of the most powerful things we can do for our health and our brains. Through the gut-brain axis, the health of our gut controls our moods, and our brain health in the long term. Supporting your gut health with probiotics can boost your overall health, longevity, and focus. Introduce organic apple cider vinegar, raw, unfiltered, and with the mother in your diet. Other vital compounds that can support gut health include L-glutamine, Pomegranate Extract, Quercetin, Vitamin D3, Vitamin B5, and Resveratrol.

Summary:

The best way to take all of these is to take a high-quality supplement that combines them so you can reduce how many pills you have to take in a day while maximizing your benefits. Since the benefits are synergistic, the benefit of combining them is exponential. Over the years we have experimented with many supplements. The most effective and highest quality supplement I have found combines most of these key herbs vitamins and minerals into a single pill making my daily routine very efficient compared to what I had to do in the past. The supplement is called Wellness from myPEAK. This supplement is formulated by physicians and until recently, it was only available from physicians. It is now available on Amazon. See below various ways to find it:

Scan with your Cell:

Visit: http://bit.ly/2wellness2
Visit: http://bit.ly/mypeakweb
Search "myPEAK Wellness" on Amazon, Etsy or eBay

I am also a big fan of their probiotic product which is better than any other probiotic on the market and does so much more than just add bacteria to your gut. I felt the difference in days. See below various ways to find it:

Scan with your Cell: 	Visit: http://bit.ly/2peakbiotic2 Visit: http://bit.ly/mypeakweb Search "myPEAK PeakBiotic" on Amazon, Etsy or eBay

These supplements check all the boxes. They are comprehensive, combine all of the ingredients I love, lists the exact doses of ingredients, is lab tested, uses trademarked ingredients, is produced in the USA at an FDA registered facility, and contains none of the toxic compounds listed earlier.

Using the right supplements, along with the right diet, water and exercise can take your performance to the next level. All this rests on a foundation of the right habits.

What are these habits?

Sleep:
Getting at least 6 hours of sleep a night (ideally 7 hours) is crucial for your ability to focus as well as feel good. While there may be periods when you sleep less and periods where you sleep more, aim to get 6-8 hours of sleep per night. This can also reduce your risk of Alzheimer's and many other chronic diseases later on in life. The following techniques will help you improve your sleep:

- Build a nightly routine to sleep from 10 pm to 6 am for optimum results.
- Eliminate mental stimuli at least 3 hours before sleep. This means avoiding all digital screens. If you must use a screen, be sure it has a nighttime blue light filter.
- Reduce or eliminate caffeine and alcohol. These two troublemakers are responsible for most of the sleep issues.
- Avoid increasing your body temperature at least 3 hours before sleep. Avoid exercise, hot showers, baths, or anything else that would increase your body temperature. A functional circadian rhythm should drop your body temperature naturally at nighttime for sleep. If it does not, you will have trouble falling asleep or staying asleep. Learn about Light therapy using a lightbox. It can help you reset your circadian rhythm.
- Designate the bedroom for sleep and lovemaking only. All other activities must be eliminated from the bedroom to properly train your brain for sleep. Approach the bed only when you are ready to sleep. Eliminate TV, electronics, blinking lights, and other distractions from the bedroom. The bedroom must be dark, quiet, and temperature-controlled to your liking.
- Expose yourself to nature and sunlight. An evening walk at sunset is very beneficial to signal the body to begin winding down for the day.
- Meditation is a must for good sleep. I recommend body-scan type meditations before sleep.

To improve your sleep, I highly recommend this wonderful book "Say Goodnight to Insomnia": https://amzn.to/36KBkpj

Exercise:
Move every day. This does not mean go to the gym. It simply means move. Go for a walk outside. Do Yoga. Garden. Rebound. Play a sport. Have fun. Do whatever you love but remember to move. Moving flushes the lymph in your body, removes toxins, and makes you feel good. Yoga

is to your body what meditation is to your mind. Just like meditation, yoga has unlimited benefits and is freely available on YouTube.

Chiropractic and Massages:

Getting regular chiropractic adjustments is a very beneficial way to eliminate blockages in your body and keep everything flowing. Each chiropractor is different. Some of them are very good. You have to find the one that works for your needs. In general, I have observed that the Joint Chiropractic (https://bit.ly/2STRYuq) network provides very affordable care with ease of walking in and out without long wait times. They already have 500+ locations around the country and growing.

Massages! Everyone loves a good spa day. Massages are very healing and eliminate blockages in your body before they become issues. Find a good-quality, affordable spa near you and enjoy it from time to time.

Connect with Nature:

Spending time outside connects you and your body to the natural rhythms of the earth. Our modern life throws off that balance by keeping us far from the earth, isolated and indoors. Nature is full of negative ions, which have uplifting benefits on your mood, the ability to reduce your blood pressure, and improve heart health. The fresh air can revitalize your lungs and the sun can provide mood upliftment alone with the essential vitamin D. Speaking of air, humans have become very good at polluting it. You can certainly invest in a good air purifier to clean the air inside your house. It definitely helps. Unfortunately, little can be done for the outside air. If your life allows it, try to live in a location where the air is more pristine and surrounded by lots of trees. New research is showing the detrimental effects of air pollution in cities on asthma, lung function, allergies, mental health, and the developing lungs of children. Every day, ground yourself by letting your bare feet touch the mother. Mother Earth that is! Your physical body is created using everything from mother earth and connecting with the mother is very healing.

Health is a personal responsibility. I have provided my opinions based on my experiences, but it is up to you to figure out what to do with this information.

If you do not take care of the body you are in, where will you live?

* * *

"*Shaak lo Bhai Shaak...*" yells the Shaakwala (produce vendor), strolling through the streets with his cart to announce his arrival. This was a common practice back in the late 80s in a small suburb of India where I grew up. The vegetables, fruits, herbs, and spices on his cart were freshly picked from his local farm. By this time of the morning, my mom would have inventoried our own garden in the backyard to see if we had enough for lunch. If not, she would buy what she needed from the Shaakwala. It was a common practice for most households in our neighborhood to have their own organically grown garden. My father was a brilliant engineer by trade but a farmer's son by birth. Many of our vegetables, herbs, and spices came from our own garden that he managed. As lunchtime approached, my mom would prepare fresh bread from scratch, starting with putting the grains in the grain mill to produce the flour.

Yes! Every household had a grain mill to make fresh flour for the bread.

The family would gather in the kitchen and sit on the stone floor in a circle around mom, in Sukhasana (lotus) position. Sitting this way stretches the muscles, improves posture, and grounds the body. Mom would serve everyone a Thali (plate) made from steel (plastic was not allowed). Everyone eats with their hands. This practice enables us to feel the texture and temperature of the food which triggers the brain to begin saliva production and prepare the body for digestion.

On a typical day, the meal would include several freshly prepared, deliciously spiced vegetables, rice of the day, Dal of the day (soup made with lentils, peas, chickpeas, beans, etc.), the bread of the day, accompanied with Chaas (buttermilk), pickle, or raita (spiced yogurt) for probiotics. There would also be Papad which would serve to clear the mouth after a meal. A typical thali would look something like this:

To the untrained mind, the ritual of sitting on the floor and eating with your hands, without a dining table, silverware, or a TV, would surely appear like poor etiquette of an undeveloped nation. However, the trained mind would see it for what it is; a tradition in harmony with the principles of Ayurveda, the world's oldest whole-body healing system, developed over 3,000 years ago and passed down thru generations in India. I remember eating the same way when we visited my grandparents.

This tradition vanished from my life as I traveled 10,000 miles away to enjoy blue jeans and beer. My wife was born in the USA and did not cook when we got married. So, we adopted the Standard American Diet (SAD) and paid the hefty price as we gained weight, became sluggish, and invited health challenges. All that changed once we started working with the UNI. One day, out of the blue, my wife was **inspired** to begin cooking. In a few short years, she became a self-taught, **inspiration-driven** expert cook and the age-old traditions returned to our home. As the nutrition returned to our bodies, our health challenges disappeared on their own. Therefore, I mean it when I say every meal is a ritual for us. Remember, when you work with the UNI, you are never deprived of the things you desire and are good for you. I emphasize the value of homemade meals because food prepared with love contains healing energies and is life-enhancing.

Today my wife is not limited to just Indian cooking, but she has combined the best of many cuisines. She has combined the old with the new, east with the west, and traditions with the technology. If you think you have to sacrifice taste to eat healthy in today's world, think again. She can make Pav Bhaji – a popular North Indian dish that takes a long time to prepare, in an instant-pot in less than half the time. Take a look at some of my wife's creations that I have been capturing. Be sure to view these pictures in color. Some of them are included below but the full album can be viewed here: http://bit.ly/meals123

Organic beet, avocado smoothie bowl with mixed berries, chia seeds, and coconut butter

Gluten-free penne with broccoli in a rich creamy vegan sauce

Indian Specialty: Pav Bhaji (Spiced mixed vegetables and gluten-free bread)

Roasted spaghetti squash topped with sautéed red cabbage, tomatoes, and guacamole

Gluten-free soba noodles with vegetables with a side of avocado and sprouts

Yellow curry ramen noodles with vegetables

Variety of energy bites made with cacao, dates, nuts, seeds, and coconut

Asian vegetable stir fry

Tricolor quinoa, roasted veggies topped with a vegan lime cilantro sauce

Indian Specialty (State of Gujarat): Spiced lentils and vegetable cakes

Gluten-free coconut flour pancakes with mixed berries

Thai yellow curry with tofu and vegetables

Fruit Medley

Gluten-free and vegan vegetable chickpea flour frittatas with a spicy garlic and cilantro sauce

Asian cashew and vegetable stir fry

I am blessed to have homes in Florida, some of which came with mature fruit trees! The climate of Florida is very supportive of gardening. Having a little produce garden of my own proved invaluable during the pandemic. If you can have your own garden, I definitely recommend creating one. When it comes to health, little changes go a long way, so, remember the old adage...

"Take care of the land, and the land will take care of you."

* * *

We spent two nights at the Hilton Head condo. The coastlines have a high concentration of negative ions, which have uplifting benefits on mood, the ability to reduce blood pressure, and improve heart health. The ocean and the sun can provide mood upliftment as well as vitamin D. We felt the calming effects of the ocean and decided to just relax the entire time. We took long walks on the beach and socialized with our friends.

"Have you guys ever been to Savannah, Georgia? It is only an hour from here and you should check it out on your way down!" said our friends as we were socializing one of the evenings.

"Here we go, the UNI speaks through its agents again," I thought, amused.

Our friends continued to describe how we would love Savannah and the many things we can do there. We instantly understood the instructions and started planning our next stop. We were happy to learn that Orlando is only a short drive away from Savannah, so we decided to stay there for the next couple of days before concluding our trip.

We enjoyed the rest of our time at the beach in Hilton Head and captured some beautiful moments with our camera.

The UNI amused us further by making a bird look like an angel.

The next day, we set sail for Savannah, GA. We arrived earlier than expected and the hotel was not ready for us so we decided to drive around. One of the first things that caught our attention was a tapestry on a wall depicting the time when Alcohol kicked America's patootie and won!

I could not help but think...

*"What would the world be like if alcohol **addiction** had been eliminated from the world?"*

13

Addictions

For the purpose of this chapter, addictions mean all habits that interfere with your UCS. These addictions include but are not limited to alcohol, smoking/vaping, illegal drugs, certain medications, caffeine, processed white sugar, etc. **Of course, some addictions create more distortion of the UCS than others and are considered more harmful.**

There is so much written about addictions, and I am not going to re-invent the wheel by going into detail about all of them here. To keep this book short, **I will use alcohol and caffeine as examples of how they impact your UCS. Please understand that all other addictions also impact your UCS in various similar ways.** Let us examine alcohol addiction.

In a medical context, alcoholism is said to exist when two or more of the following conditions are present:

- a person drinks large amounts of alcohol over a long period
- has difficulty cutting down

- acquiring and drinking alcohol takes up a great deal of time
- alcohol is strongly desired
- usage results in not fulfilling responsibilities
- usage results in social problems
- usage results in health problems
- usage results in risky situations
- withdrawal occurs when stopping
- and alcohol tolerance has occurred with the use

Alcohol use can affect all parts of the body, but it particularly affects the brain, heart, liver, pancreas, and immune system. Alcoholism can result in mental illness, delirium tremens, Wernicke–Korsakoff syndrome, irregular heartbeat, impaired immune response, liver cirrhosis, and increased cancer risk. Drinking during pregnancy can result in fetal alcohol spectrum disorders. Women are generally more sensitive than men to the harmful effects of alcohol, primarily due to their smaller body weight and lower capacity to metabolize alcohol. Warning signs of alcoholism include the consumption of increasing amounts of alcohol and frequent intoxication, preoccupation with drinking to the exclusion of other activities, promises to quit drinking and failure to keep those promises, the inability to remember what was said or done while drinking (colloquially known as "blackouts"), personality changes associated with drinking, denial or making of excuses for drinking, the refusal to admit excessive drinking, dysfunction or other problems at work or school, the loss of interest in personal appearance or hygiene, marital and economic problems, and the complaint of poor health, with loss of appetite, respiratory infections, or increased anxiety.

We are just getting warmed up. I have more scary statistics from https://bit.ly/33MzlPw and https://bit.ly/2H71YoK:

- Alcoholism reduces a person's life expectancy by approximately ten years.

- About 2 billion people across the world consume alcoholic drinks and approximately 240 million people are addicted to alcohol.
- **Globally alcohol consumption causes 2.8 million premature deaths per year.** We are so devastated by the death toll of COVID-19, yet we have ignored the much larger death toll caused by alcohol every year.
- The Global Alcoholic beverages market is accounted for $1,324.1 billion in 2017 and is expected to reach $1,864.2 billion by 2026 growing at a CAGR (Compound Annual Growth Rate) of 3.9% during the forecast period. With that kind of financial gain, life will disappear from one's body before we see alcohol disappear from our society. Remember, alcohol shamelessly kicked America's tochus in the last fight (prohibition).

The following picture depicts the effects of alcohol:

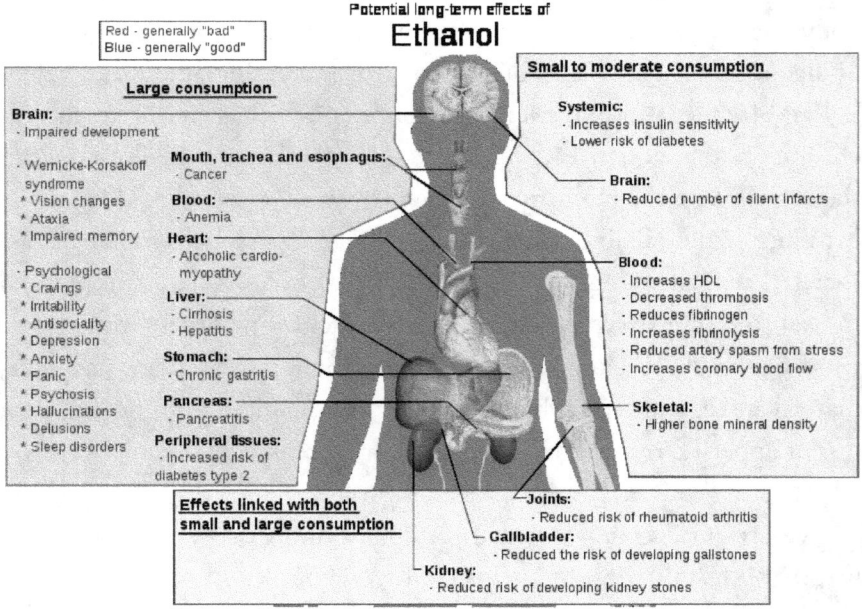

Image courtesy of Wikipedia

I think you already understand that alcohol is not your friend. I am not a stranger to alcohol myself. I grew up in a dry state in India where alcohol is prohibited. I had my first alcoholic drink as part of my professional career in America. In the corporate world, socializing with coworkers, entertaining clients and closing deals over a drink are normal practices. We all know that some aspects of drinking are enjoyable.

Who does not love the improvement in mood, the feelings of euphoria, decreased anxiety, increased self-confidence, and sociability that comes with a blood alcohol concentration (BAC) of 0.03–0.12%?

The problem is that no one really maintains the BAC between 0.03 to 0.12%. People generally keep drinking until they have reached much higher levels of BAC without even realizing it. While I drank just as normally as other corporate executives, I did not realize what it was doing to my UCS until I began working with the UNI. Please allow me to shed some light on how it distorts our UCS, intuitions, and inspirations.

Alcohol inflames our bodies and causes cellular level irritation resulting in a loss of homeostasis.

In biology, homeostasis is the state of steady internal, physical, and chemical conditions maintained by living systems. This is the condition of optimal functioning for the organism and includes many variables, such as body temperature and fluid balance, being kept within certain pre-set limits (homeostatic range). Other variables include the pH of extracellular fluid, the concentrations of sodium, potassium, and calcium ions, as well as that of the blood sugar level, and these need to be regulated despite changes in the environment, diet, or level of activity. Each of these variables is controlled by one or more regulators or homeostatic mechanisms, which together maintain life.

While we drink alcohol, the body is overwhelmed as it attempts to maintain homeostasis. **During this state, we lose the ability to understand the UCS, intuitions, and inspirations. In other words, we cannot** utilize the UNI guidance during the irritation period. This is how alcohol impairs judgment. We are no longer guided by the UNI and going through life, making decisions without the UNI. The chances of making fatal decisions are enormous during this period. At least 2,840,000 people die every year because they end up making fatal decisions without the guidance of the UNI.

The cellular irritation and the distortion of our UCS increase as we continue to drink. While the hangover lasts only for a day or two, the distortion lasts much longer.

On average, it takes about 3-10 days for the distortion to dissipate and our UCS, intuitions, and inspirations to return to normal levels. That means we are driving through life, blindfolded for 3-10 days after drinking. As one begins to meditate and reaches higher levels of awareness, one will be able to recognize the distortion more clearly. With enough mastery of meditation, one can even reduce the time it takes to recover from alcohol irritation.

There is another big problem here. **Many people drink again before the distortion has dissipated completely and thereby compounding the distortion.** Many people drink once a week. They are constantly renewing the distortion before it has a chance to dissipate completely. That means one can go through life, without utilizing the UCS, intuition, or inspirations consistently. That means one can never really create the life of one's choosing or what one creates will be unbalanced. **Unbalanced creation is a result of various addictions interfering/interrupting the creation process.** Trying to create a balanced life while having addictions is like trying to put on makeup while riding a bucking bull.

Perhaps, alcohol is one of the best examples of how media can hypnotize one into believing something that is not true. For example, the media associates alcohol with having a good time in advertisements, shows, and movies. The brain fills in the gaps and one begins to think alcohol equals a good time. With those thoughts, a new neural pathway is created. This neural pathway becomes stronger and stronger every time one sees the same information. This is why advertisements are spaced and repeated over and over again. Eventually, one forms a belief that a good time is only possible with alcohol. Once the belief is formed, one can't have a good time without alcohol. This is how subliminal programming from media impacts people. **One can be led to believe anything as long as the parameters of subconscious conditioning are followed properly.**

Caffeine:

Studies estimate that between 50 and 64% of Americans drink coffee every day, equivalent to over 150 million Americans. Caffeine, the active ingredient in coffee, is the most used drug in the United States; it is so common that it has become the norm.

But is it normal? Is it healthy?

While coffee has certain health benefits, the long-term effects of daily use can be problematic for several reasons: 1) its negative impact on your sleep 2) negative impact on cerebral (in your brain) blood flow 3) its negative impact on your UCS. Ultimately, the core cause of this is the high doses of caffeine. Caffeine works by blocking adenosine receptors in the brain.

Why is that important?

Because adenosine builds up in the brain throughout the day and causes the sensation of sleepiness and drowsiness at night and helps you go to sleep. Caffeine blocks adenosine from signaling to your brain that you are tired and ready for sleep. This does not mean you are not exhausted. If you are drinking coffee daily, you may not even know how fatigued you are because you are artificially blocking the signals your body is giving you. Any drug that blocks the natural signals of your body cuts off your connection with your UCS. And without your UCS, you are going through life blindfolded.

Furthermore, caffeine has a half-life of five hours. That means 5 hours after ingesting caffeine, you have half of that amount present in your body. Let us say you have one 8 oz cup of coffee at 5:00 PM. You get 100 mg of caffeine. At 10:00 PM, when our natural circadian rhythm and physiology is signaling that it is time to sleep through the accumulated molecule called adenosine, a rising level of melatonin (sleep hormone that begins to rise at night), and falling level of cortisol (our stress hormone), you still have 50 mg caffeine in your system. As a result, you will most likely not feel sleepy and end up staying awake much longer. Even if you go to sleep, your sleep quality will suffer, and you will wake up not feeling well-rested... needing another cup of coffee. Thus, the cycle will continue. Over the long term, this lack of restful sleep will accelerate aging, cognitive decline, and exhaust your adrenal system (decrease your ability to appropriately respond to stress).

One of the most significant impacts of caffeine is on your brain. Caffeine decreases blood flow to our brain by up to 30%. Reducing blood supply to the brain reduces the replenishment of vital oxygen in your cells as well as the detoxification of waste byproducts. Therefore, despite the artificial stimulating effect, your brain is getting less of the nourishment it needs to perform at a high level for the long term.

Lastly, and most importantly, as mentioned earlier, caffeine interferes with your UCS. When you drink caffeine, you block receptors in your brain that numb you out to your fatigue, a signal from your body to rest. **When we artificially suppress signals that our body gives us, we suppress the signals from the UCS.** Rather than taking fatigue as a sign to address something in our lives, we bury it instead and continue a vicious cycle that eventually leads us to greater and greater fatigue, dependency, and exhaustion. In addition, quitting caffeine can also reduce anxiety, reduce the appearance of wrinkles (caffeine blocks collagen formation in your skin and bones), and lower your blood pressure.

What does all this mean in practice?
Should we never drink coffee or teas or caffeinated beverages?

Not exactly. You should never NEED any of them to get rid of your fatigue or to be awake in the morning. While coffee is high in caffeine, teas such as green and white tea are loaded with healthy polyphenols and have much less caffeine. Ideally, drink decaffeinated coffee and teas and never drink either after 5 PM unless they are completely caffeine-free (like herbal teas). If the benefits of caffeine such as boosted focus, cognition, and energy are what you are seeking, I would highly recommend an amazing alternative known as theacrine. Theacrine is extracted from the Chinese Kucha Leaf and theacrine modulates adenosine receptors rather than block them, providing a much healthier effect. **With theacrine, you develop no tolerance, no anxiety, no jitters, and no crash. Even more amazing, when you take theacrine you get sustained focus, energy, and motivation that lasts for 8 hours rather than the 1-3 hours you get from caffeine AND you get better sleep at night.** The most amazing caffeine alternative I have ever tested is one called Brilliance. **It contains a clinically proven patented version of Theacrine called Teacrine®, at the studied dose of 200 mg. They combine it with another key ingredient, Cognizin®, a proven brain booster that acts as a donor of choline in the brain that improves memory and focus.** Together, these two ingredients pack a powerful natural punch that gives me focus and energy in a way that far outpaces any benefit I could get from caffeine without any of the negative effects described earlier. See below various ways to find it:

Scan with your Cell:

Visit: http://bit.ly/2brilliance2
Visit: http://bit.ly/mypeakweb
Search "myPEAK Brilliance" on Amazon, Etsy, or eBay

Now, let's discuss how to reduce, manage or eliminate addictions.

First, identify all addictions that are impacting your life and determine how addicted you are. Ask this one question to determine if you are addicted to something.

Can you go without whatever you are addicted to for at least a month?

If the answer is "No", seek professional help to eliminate your addictions. If the answer is "Yes", follow the steps below to manage/eliminate your addictions.

Let us assume your addiction is alcohol. Here is what you would do to minimize/eliminate the distortion:

- If you have strong willpower, go cold turkey, and eliminate drinking. You can also switch to non-alcoholic beer or something

beneficial like Kombucha as a replacement habit to ease into eliminating alcohol.
- If you cannot eliminate drinking, stop for at least one month. Stopping for one month is a minimum requirement because it gives your UCS, intuitions, and inspirations a chance to guide you after the irritation has dissipated (3-10 days).
- Once you have completed one month of detox, you have earned a reward of one drinking-day. You can use your reward right after you have completed one-month detox or you can save it for later. It is up to you to decide. But, as soon as you have used your reward, you must immediately begin the detox again.
- When you resume the detox, you have the option to increase the detox duration by another month. For example, the next detox cycle can be two months which will then earn you a reward of two drinking-days.
- You can increase the duration of your detox cycles or keep it the same as your last detox cycle but you can never decrease it. For example. I am on a 6-month detox cycle now. My last drink was a delicious Meadow Mule at the Big Meadows Lodge in the Shenandoah Valley. I was overlooking the gorgeous valley and enjoying my last drink when the elderly UNI agent spoke to me. I was functional and relatively sober which is why I recognized that communication from the UNI. I would have missed that communication if there had been enough distortion in my body.

- Once my 6-month detox ends, I will have earned 6 reward days.

The system outlined here has worked very well for me because it combines the best of both worlds. It provides enough distortion-free time for balanced creation. It also allows me to savor and enjoy my reward days. I generally plan my reward days when I do not have to make any important decisions. The system can be applied to all of your addictions (including media) to ensure you are allowing enough distortion-free time to create a balanced life of your choosing.

* * *

We are approaching the end of this book and our journey together. I am sure you have realized by now that it does not cost anything to begin working with the UNI. Your contract with the UNI was signed long before your birth. All you have to do is follow some rules and make some sacrifices to reap the benefits of working with the UNI. Some of these sacrifices may seem like too much. If so, it is only because you do not yet understand what a life of your choosing means. Maybe you do not fully understand the majestic nature of the UNI. Although some of you may have figured it out already, **it is time to reveal the UNI's true identity.** You already know that the UNI is more powerful than any leader, government, army, or nation. If we combine all of our human resources, we do not even come close to the capabilities of the UNI. While the powerful governments of the world struggle to cope with one pandemic, the UNI is flawlessly coordinating an unimaginable number of variables, events, and circumstances to produce the most precise co-creative experience for all that is! The UNI is the most powerful and the most wonderful friend you will ever have. If you have the UNI by your side, you will never need another political leader to rescue you!

To get a glimpse of such coordination, I would like you to wind down tonight with a sleep story called "Wonder". The story follows a grandfather as he explains the magic of the UNI to his granddaughter. The story is read by Matthew McConaughey with his charming accent and smooth as silk voice. Many of you will not make it to the end of this soothing story and fall asleep sooner. It is okay to fall asleep before the end. Just listen to it again and again until you begin to fathom and appreciate the magic of the UNI.

Are you ready?

First, be sure to turn off the "Autoplay" setting in your YouTube app to prevent it from playing the next video automatically, which could ruin your relaxing experience. Then, get in the bed, put on your headset, and browse to this link: https://bit.ly/30MXxz2 or search YouTube for "Matthew McConaughey Wonder || Sleep Story Relaxation Meditation".

14

Brahma Shakti

Brahma Shakti is the ultimate cosmic energy of creation. Brahma Shakti is a combination of two Sanskrit (the oldest language) words. According to ancient Indian sacred texts, Brahma (pronounced: Brahmā) is the creator of the universe, and Shakti (pronounced: Śhakti) is the primordial cosmic energy used for all creation in the universe.

Creation is why we are here on planet earth, playing the video game of life. The job of the UNI is to help us with that creation. If we utilize our UCS, intuitions, and inspirations properly, we can mold the Brahma Shakti to our liking and create what we want with joy! Just like a sculptor molds the clay to create a masterpiece, you will now learn how to mold Brahma Shakti to create the life of your choosing.

Most people are not taught how to mold Brahma Shakti by their family, friends, or teachers and they have not deliberately molded Brahma Shakti before. Most people probably do not have years to waste. Therefore, this chapter will outline a daily process to create your dream life as quickly as possible. Over the years, I have tried and tested many processes that mold the Brahma Shakti. However, the one I am going to teach you now is my absolute favorite because it is the most powerful and the most fun.

The process involves writing letters to the UNI. I call them "Dear Friend" letters. At a minimum, these rules must be followed while writing the letters:

- The letter must be handwritten. Typing is not allowed.
- The letter should be written on white blank paper with preferably a blue pen. If not available, then electronic devices that allow handwriting on the screen with a pen-like instrument can be used as a substitute.
- The letter must be detailed enough and include what, when, where, who, how, and why elements. If it is not possible to include all elements, then include as many of them as possible.
- The letter must include details that evoke Fan-14 or preferably Fab-5 while being written. **Anything that does not evoke Fan-14 must be avoided.**
- Your focus must be on the positive and never on the negative. For example, "I want to be healthier..." is allowed but "I do not want to be sick anymore..." is not allowed.
- Spend as much time writing the letter as possible. The longer the better.
- Perform this exercise consistently. Consistency is key.
- If you are writing a letter to create something you want but do not have, write it as if what you want has already happened and you are just reporting the details of how it happened.

I will now include two examples of "Dear Friend" letters.

***

Type: Gratitude Letter.
Purpose: Allows you to create more of what you already like about

your life. **Prevents negative pull from expanding further on all topics where you have negative pull and even reduces it on topics where you have not reached the destroyer size.**

Tips: Be as detailed as possible and passionately feel the emotions as you recall and write about the things you appreciate.

Sample:

Dear Friend,

I know you love reading about all that is good in my life. I am so excited to outline just a few of the so many things I love about my life, so far...

I love falling asleep in my bed. The bed is so soft and feels like I am sleeping on the clouds. I love that I can control the firmness of the mattress. I love using the massager to soothe my body. I love that I can adjust the bed to any angle. I love to elevate my head and legs just to my liking to promote sleeping on my back. I am so happy that I am sleeping on my back more and more every day. I love that my body heals better while I sleep on my back with proper elevation. I love that my bed is such a wonderful place for comfort, rest, relaxation, joy, and healing. I love that my wife is right next to me. I love that she can adjust her side of the bed to her liking as well. I love that the bed is big enough for both of us and has a split top so we can both have our space. I love the softness of the bamboo sheets. I love that dual-purpose pillow. I love that one side keeps my head cooler in the summer and the other keeps it warmer in the winter. I love how soft and ergonomic the pillow is. I love how nicely it supports my head. I love the soft light under the bed. It is useful when I get up at night and turns off while I sleep. I love that the entire bed is crafted carefully with organic and healthy materials. I love that the bed is positioned perfectly so that my head is facing east while sleeping. I love that I sleep well in this bed. I love that my body always feels refreshed after each night of sleep. I love how excited I am at the beginning of every morning. What a wonderful bed! What a healing place! Thank you, Thank you, Thank you for this wonderful bed!

and so on...
***

That appreciation was just for my bed to give you a sample of how the letter is written. A complete letter would include all aspects of your life that are pleasing to you and will be a lot longer

You already know that what you focus on expands. **It is important to understand that the process of handwriting engages all parts of your being to focus.**

Have you ever used a magnifying glass to concentrate solar energy onto a tiny spot?

If so, you understand the power of concentrated energy. The process of handwriting allows you to focus intensely and intently. **Just like a magnifying glass concentrates solar energy, your focus concentrates the Brahma Shakti directly upon whatever you are writing about. Therefore, what you are writing about will begin to expand and eventually manifest.** The process of handwriting is one of the best ways to deliberately mold the Brahma Shakti into the life of your choosing.

Let us look at an example of writing a letter to create something you want but do not have. You must write the letter as if what you want has already happened and you are just reporting the details of how it happened to your dear friend, the UNI.

***
Type: Manifestation Letter.
Purpose: Allows you to create something you want but do not yet have.

Tips: If you are uncertain of the details of "how" what you want will manifest, be general in your description. Write more about how you felt when you got what you wanted. Write more about the things you did and the fun you had instead of how something manifested unless you are very confident about the "how".

Sample:

Dear Friend,

I know you love reading about all that is good in my life. I have to tell you about the easiest $50,000 I have ever made...

It all started when I made $50,000 with ease! Here I was going about my life, doing the things I do and tada...$50,000 just fell in my lap through a series of fortuitous circumstances that made me go...WOW! It felt so good to have this money that I did not even need. Let me tell you what I did with that money.

You know how much we love traveling. We started planning a trip immediately. The process of planning the trip felt much easier because of the free money. We decided to go to Aruba. We booked an elite-class flight and picked the desired time so we would not have to wake up early.

We woke up at our usual time and leisurely got ready. It was a cold winter morning in Princeton, NJ. Soon after we were ready, we saw the limousine pull up at the driveway. Perfect timing! We did not have our breakfast because we had better plans! The driver picked up our luggage and held the door open while we slipped into the stretch limo. We felt the chill walking to the limo and were very happy to be going away to a warm paradise. The limo was nice and warm with a little snack station set up including champagne. We enjoyed the fresh fruits, cheese, and crackers on our way to the airport. It seemed like a very short ride to the airport and we couldn't stop chatting about all the things we would do when we get to Aruba. The sun, the sand, the music, the dancing, the food, and the freedom to do whatever we want for the next two weeks!

I loved the chauffeur service offered by the airline. They checked us in and took our luggage without us having to wait in any lines. We were escorted directly to the lounge. We found ourselves a good seat by the window and put in our complimentary breakfast orders. My wife made us plates of hors d'oeuvres while we waited for the gourmet breakfast to arrive. This airline offered one of the best lounge services including several complete bars, restaurants, buffet stations, private offices, showers, day beds, spa, salon, and more. All services were complimentary. While we enjoyed our delicious Michelin-Star-Chef-inspired breakfast, a very polite young lady approached us for our spa treatment. We signed up for a side-by-side treatment and enjoyed it thoroughly. There is nothing better than a loose-as-a-goose body before getting on a flight.

We were notified when the flight was ready for us. We walked aboard and sat down in our comfortable chairs. After breakfast and the massage, we were both ready for our meditation. Right after the hot towel and the champagne service, we put on our headsets and started meditation.

When I came out of meditation, almost two hours had passed. I felt refreshed and excited! I got up and walked to the bar/lounge to stretch my legs. There were a few happy and chatty people already at the bar. One of them had been to Aruba many times and owned a place on the beach. It did not take long for him to spill the beans on the best of Aruba. My wife walked in and joined just as he was beginning his virtual tour of Aruba. Just 30 minutes with this guy and we knew exactly what we wanted to do for the next two weeks. He even invited us to his house. We shared the contact details and were ready for the next activity, movies!

The movie library contained hits that were just released in theaters.

We had enough entertainment to keep us busy for the rest of the flight. Before starting the movies, we decided to put in our food and drink orders. We looked at the full-size menu and put in our meal orders. Of course, all meals, drinks, and entertainment are complimentary for the elite class.

Time flies when you are having fun. Just as I finished my movie, we were about to land. We looked outside the window and saw the breathtaking beauty of this perfect sized island surrounded by the turquoise Caribbean Sea. Perfect beaches, crystal clear warm water, variety of food, water sports, natural-pool, 4x4 off-roading, prehistoric pictographs, Divi trees, wild-life, and more...The best part was the budget of $50,000...Aruba, get ready...for the King and the Queen have arrived!

and so on...
***

The sample above is only an excerpt from a long letter that described the complete two-week trip. I wrote this letter not long before the $50,000 arrived. The first time I wrote the letter, I could not even formulate one paragraph. Therefore, the letters were very general in the beginning and only described the overall feeling of having received $50,000 with ease. As the days went by, my neural pathways became stronger and stronger and so did the magnetic pull associated with them. It became easier and easier to write these letters with more and more details as the Law of Focus flooded my thoughts with more and more similar details. Taking that trip virtually while writing the letter became so pleasurable that I would find myself completely immersed in the experience until something tuned me out. One day, what tuned me out was the knock on the door that brought the $50,000!

I know with certainty that many will go directly to the Dear Friend

Manifestation Letter (DFML) and start writing about the long list of things not yet achieved. **And that is where things can go wrong!**

One must learn how to walk before one jumps. It is our nature to crave the things desired but not yet achieved. **When we crave what we do not have, we are focused incorrectly and our UCS fires a warning bell.** It takes time, practice and experience to differentiate UCS warning bells, intuitions, and inspirations. The difference is very subtle. **The UCS warning bells are always in response to incorrect thoughts/focus while intuitions and inspirations are not. The intuitions are downloads from the UNI to guide us correctly and inspirations are intuitions that require action in due time.** Writing a DFML before one can differentiate UCS, intuitions, and inspirations; is risky because it can keep what one wants away even longer.

But I need the money now!!!

You do not have to wait too long to begin manifesting what you want. You can start with the Dear Friend Gratitude Letter (DFGL) first. Do not underestimate the power of DFGL. There is so much more to it than one may realize.

All of us have the neural pathways already in place for the emotions of gratitude and appreciation. It is so because all of us have experienced those emotions before. These neural pathways may be weak, but it is so easy to strengthen them by repetition and expand the positive pull simultaneously. **With every iteration of the DFGL, you will expand the positive pull of all topics in your life simultaneously and also stop/reduce the expansion of the negative pull for topics where you have not reached the destroyer-size pull yet.** In other words, the DFGL is a cure-all solution when you first begin working with the UNI. As you increase the positive pull of all topics with the DFGL, so many amazing things will automatically begin manifesting in your life. Even today, the majority of the time, I am only writing the DFGL. The DFML is only reserved for special situations. Once you have worked with the UNI for long enough, you will be **inspired** to switch to the DFML when you are ready.

Am I suggesting that all you have to do is write these letters and things will fall in your lap?

No. Please allow me to explain. We live in a world where we are taught to work hard. We are led to believe only hard work can produce results. Yet, some of the hardest working people I know are not doing so well in terms of health, wealth, or happiness while some others that aren't working as hard, are doing fantastic! In reality, the best results are achieved when our focus is perfected first and then work is performed in the direction of that perfected focus. **There are two parts to all creation, the first is the molding of the energy and the second is allowing the manifestation of that molded energy in our reality through inspired actions.** If you recall, Jenna and Jack molded energy with their negative focus first which then resulted in the negative manifestation of a fight and ultimately a divorce. To manifest positive results, we must mold energy by correcting our focus first. This is the most important part of creation. This is what you can accomplish with DFGL and DFML. Once you have perfected your focus and molded energy to your liking, intuitions and inspirations will guide you to the actions leading to manifestation. **Yes, you have to work to manifest things in life but it does not feel like work when actions are inspired and leading to manifest what you desire.** For example, when my millions showed up, it required work to get that money into a bank account. It took weeks of tough negotiations and legal paperwork before the money moved into a bank account. I can assure you it didn't feel like work because I wanted the millions and was inspired to do the work that would move that money into the bank account.

* * *

"Why don't we sign up for one of those tours to see the town. Maybe we can *do that after lunch."* said my wife. We had decided to have lunch while we waited for the room to be ready in Savannah, GA. We picked "Naan on Broughton" for lunch. Restaurants were allowed to open just recently after a long pandemic related shutdown, and we were the only ones in the restaurant. We could feel the warmth in how our server greeted us. Needless to say, we got the royal treatment and he even made me a custom Indian-style masala soda. I love how the pandemic has strengthened the business-customer mutual appreciation.

Just as we exited the restaurant, I saw a tour bus passing by, and then came the **inspiration...**

"Why don't we just follow the tour bus?" whispered the UNI, in my head.

"Thank you, UNI. We are going to follow the tour bus, see what they see, and stop where they stop..." I announced to my wife. We both laughed with excitement and started following the tour bus in our vehicle. We rolled down the windows and could hear the open-window-trolly guide loud and clear. The bus went to square after square, site after site and stopped at the Cathedral Basilica of St. John the Baptist, a 19th-century Roman Catholic church with neo-gothic architecture, stained glass, and music recitals. The UNI signal is especially strong in places of worship and we would not miss a chance to pray. Besides, it was a beautiful sunny day and we could not wait to see the stained glass from the inside.

After that prayer, we felt comforted and knew that Savannah was going to be a great experience. We followed the trolly to our heart's content until the hotel notified us that our room was ready. At that point, we checked into the boutique hotel and marveled at our room on the top floor. The hotel was well-decorated and relatively empty. The location was central with the historic districts on one side and the river on the opposite side. The best part was the soft bed which reminded us of our bed at home.

After a rejuvenating meditation, we were ready to explore Savannah on foot. We decided to explore the city's squares for the rest of the evening and save the riverside for the next day.

We strolled back to the hotel in the cool of the night. As we lay in bed that night, the sky lit up with fireworks! We watched the show from our bed and fell asleep soon after.

Thank you, UNI, for your perfect timing.

For dinner, we picked the Flying Monk Noodle Bar and had a delicious meal.
Image courtesy of Google

15

Eternal Peace

The pandemic is here and it will stay around as long as the majority of the people continue to focus on it. The same is true for political upheaval, civil unrest, and chaos. The best way to cease these terrible conditions is by focusing away from them or focusing on the solution, not the problem.

Can we get the majority of the people to refocus correctly?

That depends on whether or not they choose to disconnect from the media and begin to focus on things that feel good. The good news is that your reality and experiences do not depend on how others have focused. As I have shown you through the examples of my road trip during the pandemic, your experience can be wonderful regardless of what is going on in the world around you. **It is only your focus that determines your reality and your experience.** In today's world, many people work with the UNI and for them, life is delicious. They are in the right place at the right time and the UNI always protects, guides, and provides for them. While the majority of humanity suffered, the total wealth of the US Billionaires grew to over $4,000,000,000,000 (4 Trillion) during the pandemic! For so many, this was the year of opportunities and they benefited from the economic stimulus packages, record-breaking prices for stocks, cryptocurrencies, gold, and more. The fact is, 2020 was a wonderful year for everyone that works with the UNI and not just the Billionaires. Master how to work with the UNI and you too will find yourself in the right place at the right time even during global turmoil.

I am well aware that many people will not understand the esoteric wisdom contained here. What you get out of this book will depend on how ready you are. If you felt good overall and even got occasional goosebumps while reading the book, you can process this wisdom correctly and your results will be amazing. If the book annoyed, upset, or offended you then you experienced UCS warning bells indicating incorrect thoughts, focus, and conditioning. Please be aware that millions have been exposed to the Law of Attraction (Law of Focus) over the last decade. While it does not resonate with everyone, so many have already changed their lives using this knowledge. More and more people are starting to work with the UNI every day! Even if this information does not resonate with you, your life can still improve to the extent you practice what is taught here.

You have not learned everything about the UNI yet, but you have learned enough to create the life of your choosing. Let us summarize what you have learned.

You now understand how the Law of Focus works and you have it memorized like your own name.
What you focus on expands.
What you focus on with your five senses; touch, sight, smell, taste, and hearing; expands.
What you focus on with your thoughts, expands.
What you focus on with your emotions, expands.
What you focus on, with any part of your being, expands.
What you focus on with one or more parts of your being, expands.

The more parts you involve in your focus, the faster it expands.

As you get more beings to focus, the expansion becomes exponential.

The expansion has an energetic pull, like gravity or magnets.

The bigger the expansion, the stronger the pull.

You now understand how this supreme law manages all that is and all that happens to you, your family, your neighborhood, your city, your county, your state, your country, your world, your solar system, your galaxy, and your **universe.**

You know for a fact that your body is already equipped with the UNI Communications System (UCS) and has tons of safety features with bells and whistles. These bells and whistles have been firing your entire life, to prevent you from making mistakes and to ensure you have only the best experiences in life.

Every time you focus on something, UCS notifies you whether it is good for you or not.

Every time you think a thought, UCS notifies you whether it is good for you or not.

Every time you make a decision, UCS notifies you whether it is good for you or not.

Every time you take an action, UCS notifies you whether it is good for you or not.

And so on...

You understand that once you begin thinking about what you are focused upon, emotions will ensue soon after. You now know that the emotions are either positive, negative, or neutral/ambiguous depending on your exact thoughts regarding what you are focused upon. You understand the difference between Fab-5, Fan-14, and Nasty-9 and you have them memorized:

Fab-5 : (Joy/Appreciation/Empowerment/Freedom/Love)

Fan-14 : (Joy/Appreciation/Empowerment/Freedom/Love, Passion, Enthusiasm/Eagerness/Happiness, Positive Expectation/Belief, Optimism, Hopefulness, Contentment)

Nasty-9 : (Revenge, Hatred, Rage, Jealousy, Fear, Grief, Desperation, Despair, or Powerlessness)

You have learned that negative emotions are only meant to be temporary warning bells and you will not dwell on negative emotions. You have learned to correct your focus. You understand that correcting your focus requires turning one or more parts of your being away from the cause of the disturbance and refocusing them differently until you feel one of the Fan-14.

You understand how your focus creates expansion which has a magnetic pull. You have made a list of topics with various positive or negative pull. You have tried Thought Field Therapy to eliminate negative pull or stayed away from topics where you have a destroyer size negative pull. You are now willing to follow some rules and make some sacrifices to joyfully create the life of your choosing. You clearly understand how your UCS, intuitions, inspirations, and free will work together to create the life of your choosing. You now know that you can be, do, or have anything as long as you master the awareness of your UCS, intuitions, and inspirations. You understand that everything you want in life can be achieved with your ability to focus correctly! You also understand how the UNI coordinates people, circumstances, events, and more, involving all living beings as necessary to create the life of your choosing. You now understand the difference among UCS warning bells, intuitions, and inspirations. The UCS warning bells are always in response to incorrect thoughts/focus while intuitions and inspirations are not. The intuitions are downloads from the UNI to guide you correctly and inspirations are intuitions that require action in due time.

You understand the immense power of meditation and you realize that nothing can enhance your intuitions and inspirations better than meditation. You are now meditating regularly and reaping the benefits from it.

You understand hypnosis. You now know that hypnosis occurs when you accept information as truth, without vetting it first. You understand that you need to be extra careful about the hypnosis coming from the sources you trust. You understand these sources include family, teachers, friends, religious leaders, political leaders, authority figures, newspapers, magazines, radio, television, music, internet, cell phones, computers, tablets, anything with internet connectivity, email, texting, messengers, social media, streaming services, and more. You realize that the leaders of today are masters of persuasion and it is dangerous to become a pawn in their game of thrones.

You are now aware that the media can easily condition you to believe things that are not true. They have the technology, resources, and wherewithal to do so and most of the media is used for hypnotizing you in a harmful way. You realize the limitation that humans cannot fact-check all the content that is generated every day. You also know that you are already equipped with something that does fact-check everything. The UNI already knows what, when, where, who, how, and why of all media content and can alert you through your UCS.

You understand that many of your thoughts are a result of the media stimulus and you cannot separate the intuitions and inspiration from that pile of garbage unless you eliminate the media. Therefore, you have started your media detox to wash away a lifetime worth of false beliefs. You are now choosing your thoughts deliberately to create the life of your dreams with rapid speed!

Furthermore, you understand that any media content you consume in the future must evoke a Fab-5 from you!

You have learned about opinions and approval through the story of the elephant and the blind men. You understand that your senses do not interpret reality as it truly is and you have accepted the fact that our opinions are not meant to be imposed on others. You have eliminated virtually all your suffering just by not imposing your opinions on others. Now that you understand opinions, you do not let the opinions of others bother you either. Therefore, you have already achieved lasting peace.

You also understand that your need for approval is invalid. You have identified and eliminated any habits that require the approval of others. You understand very clearly that approval of your UCS is the only approval you need!

You understand how dangerous addictions are. You understand that all habits that interfere with your UCS, intuitions, and inspirations are considered addictions. These addictions include but are not limited to alcohol, smoking/vaping, illegal drugs, certain medications, caffeine, sugar, and more. You do not wish to go through life without the help of the UNI. Therefore, you have made plans to manage or eliminate your addictions.

You have embarked on a journey to improve your physical and mental health. You are drinking water that is properly prepared and heals your body. You have learned all names for MSG and HFCS and eliminated them from your diet. You buy organic and have eliminated pesticides, harmful chemicals, artificial sweeteners, gluten, and dairy. You have reduced or eliminated meat usage. You have cleaned your diet and vitalized your body with fruits, vegetables, nuts, healthy oils, healthy grains, lentils, and beans. You understand the value of good supplements. You have eliminated any supplements with magnesium stearate, stearic acid, gelatin, propylene glycol, aspartame, sucralose, GMOs, vanillin, EDTA, and FD&C food colors. You have learned about the life-enhancing effects of vitamin D3, B-complex, alpha-GPC, resveratrol, astaxanthin, and probiotics. You have now introduced supplements to your diet to take your abilities to another level.

You have also taken measures to sleep well. You sleep well and your sleep is refreshing and energizing. You also exercise, get chiropractic adjustments, and massages regularly. You have connected with nature and are appreciating the wonders of this beautiful planet.

You have now harnessed the power of creation. You understand how to mold Brahma Shakti to create the life of your choosing. You understand the power of the gratitude letters and you are writing them regularly. You also understand the difference between the DFGL and the DFML and you know how to use each one properly.

Finally, through the examples of the road trip, I have taught you how to **be** and **do** so you can **have** the life of your choosing.

Of course, I am assuming that you have either already incorporated or will incorporate into your life that which you have learned from this book. **Anyone can work with the UNI. However, only the ones with honesty, courage, and consistency will have remarkable results.**

Honesty:
You must be honest about what the UCS is telling you. When you get that urge to criticize that awful politician or scream at a loved one or lift that finger to declare your feelings to the driver that cut you off, be honest about what the UCS is telling you. A warning bell is a warning bell and it simply means you need to refocus correctly regardless of how you have been wronged.

Courage:
It takes courage to stop yourself when the urge to criticize, scream, or lift that finger is so strong. It takes courage to give up addictions. It

takes courage to give up media. It takes courage to do things differently, think differently, do away with opinions, and the need for approval. It takes courage to be different than the rest of the world and still be proud.

Consistency:
Consistency is the key. Apply what you have learned consistently for the rest of your life and you will see the magic unfold. Also, make it a habit to read this book 4 times a year.

Why?

Because our brains do not capture everything we read for the first time. The brain will capture only what it can process during the first iteration. Then allow a few months to build new neural pathways and read the book again. You will now be able to capture additional information missed during the first iteration. This is the reason why we find new scenes when watching the same movie again. **Repetition is the key.** Repetition of good habits is how we build strong neural pathways with strong positive pull. When that positive pull reaches the tipping point, magic happens!

Your results will speak the truth.

You are born to be amazing. You are designed for success. You came here to create a life of your choosing with joy. You are not alone and you never will be alone. You came equipped with a direct connection to the most powerful entity there is. The entire purpose of the UNI is to support and guide you so that you can fulfill all of your dreams and desires. So, let go of your fears and rise like the majestic mountain you are. Go forth and conquer this world and have fun doing it!

Congratulations! You have now graduated from the UNI (versity) of the **UNI**(VERSE). You now know how to work with the **UNIVERSE** and the entire **UNIVERSE** is at your service!

What will you do with this infinite cosmic power?

* * *

The next day we started our exploration on the riverside of Savannah. The riverside has quite a different charm than the squares. Our day started with some pandemic humor as we passed by a funny sign.

We loved walking down to the historic steps that descend from the higher elevation of the city to the lower level next to the river. At this level, you have a historic street with small, unique shops on one side and the river on the other side. We enjoyed exploring these unique shops.

I almost tried the legendary saltwater taffy, but it contained neither salt nor water.

We then came across a monument that caught our attention. After I took the picture, I moved in closer to read the inscription.

> "We were stolen, sold, and bought together from the African continent. We got on the slave ships together. We lay back to belly in the holds of the slave ships in each others' excrement and urine together, sometimes died together, and our lifeless bodies thrown overboard together. Today, we are standing up together, with faith and even some joy."
>
> -Maya Angelou

WOW!

I felt the weight of those words and the pain behind them. The George Floyd event had taken place recently and the country was still plagued with not just the pandemic but also the violent riots. I had to sit down and ponder why we are unable to find peace. I wondered if I should share what we know with the world to make it a better place.

"Are you waiting for the underground railroad tour?" asked the elderly Caucasian couple as they approached us, wondering if we were waiting for the same tour they were looking for.

"No. We were just thinking about that monument." I replied.

The friendly couple started chatting with us and the conversation took a natural turn in the direction of the pandemic matters. In the back of my mind, I was still thinking about the inscription. I am generally not interested in voicing my opinion, but on this occasion, I could not help but speak about how the minds of the masses have been manipulated to give birth to such chaos. Impressed with my explanation, the couple asked if I were a psychologist.

"I am not a psychologist, but I have learned enough to write a book about it," I replied passionately, and the goosebumps rippled through my body.

And that is how it happened!

The UNI not only inspired me to write this book, but the inspiration was so strong that the words leaped out of my mouth, followed by the UCS approval with goosebumps.

And did you notice the couple that showed up at the right time to facilitate the co-creation leading to the inspiration?

We had lunch at Namaste Savannah. Once again, it was just us in the restaurant. To meet our vegan diet requirements, the owner made us an off the menu fusion item and we loved it!

For the rest of the day, we explored the riverside of Savannah with a deep appreciation for its history.

All that walking made us very hungry, so we headed out to find something special for our last road trip dinner. We selected Kayak Kafe because it caters to the vegan and gluten-free community.

The UNI knew this was our last dinner before we head back home tomorrow morning. So, it went the extra mile to please us. First, the UNI surprised us with my favorite Kombucha brand, Buchi. Then the UNI surprised us with their in-house spicy yellow sauce. It was not just delicious but had such a spicy kick that hit-the-spot perfectly. Just as we finished the meal, the UNI put the cherry on the top. It showed us a rainbow which has a very special meaning for us.

The rainbow represents personal symbolism between the UNI and us (my wife and I). Once you have worked with the UNI for some time, you will automatically recognize your symbolism with the UNI. Whether it is a specific bird, animal, number, song, or something else, you will know when you see it repeatedly. It will show up at important points in your life. The UNI presents us with rainbows at important points in our lives. It means,

> "I am watching over you and everything is well. Let this be a reminder that I will always watch over you and everything will always be well for you."

We wanted to take a final stroll on the riverside after dinner to say our goodbyes. It was still raining, and we needed it stopped so we can leave the restaurant. With the knowingness that the UNI was listening to our thoughts, we asked it to stop the rain and it complied. I was not joking when I said weather management is one of the perks of working with the UNI.

We stopped by the riverside and said our goodbyes to the beautiful city of Savannah, Georgia and our road-trip. It was a heartfelt bitter-sweet moment.

My heart was filled with gratitude that night as we spooned. We set out on this road-trip in the middle of a raging pandemic and riots. The state of New York was the worst hit at that time and it happened to be our destination. The world was experiencing a full-blown panic attack with confusion, chaos, and division at every turn. The leaders of the world were caught with their pants down. While the governments of the world struggled to contain the pandemic, we hit the road with peace, tranquility, and excitement. We had complete belief in the UNI and its ability to protect us on our journey across almost 3,000 miles, 10 states, and 10 overnight stops. We had laughs and made memories with family and friends. We visited forests, caverns, bridges, lakes, bays, oceans, mountains, valleys, rivers, waterfalls, and monuments. We were presented with clear roads, courteous drivers, delicious food, beautiful weather, fresh air, and nature. We interacted with humans, cows, goats, horses, and birds. That is all it takes to be happy. **Focusing correctly is all that is needed to find happiness during a Pandemic!**

As we were falling asleep, I thought about the monument again and my inspiration to write a book. I had never written a book, let alone written one in English. English is my fourth language, and I learned it by reading newspapers and looking up words I did not understand. Despite my lack of experience as a writer and the language barrier, I knew deep inside that I was going to **follow-through on my inspiration.**

I started writing the very next day and here we are! The candid pictures from the road trip provided the foundation for the book and the UNI inspired the ideas and the words to complete the rest of the book.

I have done my part by showing you how to work with the UNI to achieve health, wealth, happiness, prosperity, peace, or anything else you desire regardless of what is going on in the world around you.

The rest is up to you.

* * *

P.S.

I finished writing this book on the afternoon of September 16, 2020. It was a milestone for me. That evening, my wife and I drove to Kelly

Park, Merritt Island to enjoy our evening and reflect on the journey of writing this book. When we arrived, there was a message in the sky, from the UNI, for all of us...

> *"I am watching over you and everything is well. Let this be a reminder that I will always watch over you and everything will always be well for you."*

Origin
Authors
Date taken   9/16/2020 5:25 PM
Program name   N960USQS5ETH2

Epilogue

To keep this book short and to the point, I did not go into the details of certain topics. For those interested in learning more regarding such topics, check out the work of some incredible authors below.

It is with great pleasure I recommend the work of Abraham Hicks. While I learned about the Law of Attraction elsewhere, I cannot think of a better teacher of the Law of Attraction than Abraham. In my opinion, Esther and Jerry Hicks, bringing forth the wisdom of the UNI, was the most significant event in the history of mankind. Their books are a publishing milestone and a must-read.

The Vortex: Where the Law of Attraction Assembles All Cooperative Relationships
Money, and the Law of Attraction
Manifest Your Desires: 365 Ways to Make Your Dream a Reality
The Astonishing Power of Emotions: Let Your Feelings Be Your Guide
The Law of Attraction: The Basics of the Teachings of Abraham
The Amazing Power of Deliberate Intent: Finding the Path to Joy Through Energy Balance
Ask and It Is Given: Learning to Manifest Your Desires

Also, for those looking for additional proof that the UNI exist, please read Pam Grout's E-Squared: 9 Do-it-Yourself Energy Experiments That Prove Your Thoughts Create Your Reality. Additional recommendations as follows:

The Untethered Soul: The Journey Beyond Yourself
The Power of Now
A Happy Pocket Full of Money
A New Earth
Thank & Grow Rich

Mitesh Patel is a visionary entrepreneur, investor, and mentor to many.

Mitesh's professional career spans several decades and includes managing large-scale global projects to developing cutting-edge technologies to building companies from the ground up.

Using the concepts described in the book, Mitesh went from being homeless to a successful entrepreneur and retired before the age of 40. Mitesh was recognized as one of the Top 50 Successful Indian Entrepreneurs in the USA in 2017 and as one of the Top 10 Value Added Service Providers in 2018. Mitesh's companies have served clients as large as Fortune 500 corporations, Small and Medium Businesses, and even celebrities.

www.ingramcontent.com/pod-product-compliance
Lightning Source LLC
Chambersburg PA
CBHW071825080526
44589CB00012B/920